ZIONISM

Its Role in World Politics

by HYMAN LUMER

INTERNATIONAL PUBLISHERS New York

To Dorothy

Copyright by HYMAN LUMER 1973
ALL RIGHTS RESERVED
First Edition, 1973
ISBN 0-7178-0383-X
Library of Congress Catalog Card Number: LC 72-94393
Printed in the United States of America

CONTENTS

3

4

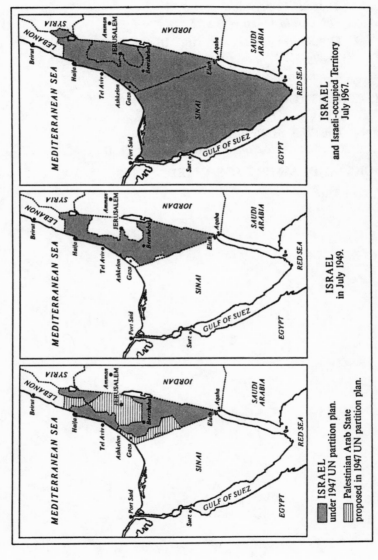

ISRAEL
under 1947 UN partition plan.

Palestinian Arab State
proposed in 1947 UN partition plan.

ISRAEL
and Israeli-occupied Territory
July 1967.

ISRAEL
in July 1949.

I

WHAT IS ZIONISM?

1. THE NATURE AND ROOTS OF ZIONISM

Origins of Political Zionism

The prolonged crisis in the Middle East, beginning with the events of May 1967 and the ensuing Israeli-Arab war, has brought the question of Zionism very sharply to the fore. It is Zionism which underlies the policies of the Israeli government, and which motivates the main body of its supporters in the United States and other capitalist countries. Hence, to understand fully the nature of the conflict between Israel and the Arab states, as well as the political and social orientation of the major Jewish organizations and spokesmen in this country, it is necessary to examine in some detail the nature of Zionism and its role in the present-day world.

Political Zionism, whose aim is the creation and perpetuation of a Jewish state, had its origins in the last decades of the 19th century, animated by the upsurge of anti-Semitism in Europe which accompanied the rise of modern imperialism. It is quite distinct from the older religious Zionism—the belief in an eventual return to the Holy Land upon the coming of the Messiah.

Its chief forerunner was Moses Hess, who for a number of years had been an associate of Karl Marx. But he later became an ardent Jewish nationalist, and in his book *Rome and Jerusalem,* published in 1862, he expounded such ideas as these: "We Jews shall always remain strangers among the nations. . . . Each and every Jew, whether he wishes it or not, is automatically, by virtue of his birth, bound in solidarity with his entire nation. . . . Each has the solidarity and responsibility for the rebirth of Israel." But at the time

these ideas met with little response and nothing further came of
them. The rise of political Zionism as a movement was to come
somewhat later.

The two classical presentations of the Zionist doctrine are Leo
Pinsker's *Auto-Emancipation* (1882) and Theodor Herzl's *The
Jewish State* (1896).

Pinsker's book grew out of the sharply intensified persecution of
the Jews in tsarist Russia in 1881, signalized by a wave of pogroms
in Kishinev and other localities and by the imposition of a mass of
discriminatory legislation, including confinement to ghettos. Shortly
afterward, in 1884, there was launched in Odessa the Chovevei
Zion (Lovers of Zion), a society dedicated to the establishment of
Jewish settlements in Palestine.

It is Herzl, however, who is considered the founder of modern
political Zionism. An assimilated Austrian Jew, he was deeply
shocked by the anti-Semitic frameup of Captain Alfred Dreyfus in
France in 1894, which he covered as a journalist. It was this which
led him to develop the doctrine of Zionism, entirely independently
of Pinsker and other predecessors, and to devote himself to its ful-
fillment.

Thus the emergence of Zionism corresponds to a new upsurge of
anti-Semitism, associated with the rise of modern imperialism and
its extreme development of racism as an ideological instrument of
oppression. It was a new type of anti-Semitism, not primarily rooted
in religious bigotry as in the past, but essentially secular and racial
in character. The historian S. M. Dubnow describes it as follows:

> The last quarter of the xixth century saw a new anti-Jewish move-
> ment in Europe. It went by the name of "anti-Semitism" and resolved
> itself into an attempt to revive the old Jew-baiting practices of the Mid-
> dle Ages under a new disguise. The rapid progress the Jews, once
> emancipated, had made in all fields of social and industrial activity had
> aroused the jealous fear of those sections of Christian society which still
> clung to the idea of the social inferiority of the Hebrew people. It was
> declared that the Jew, being a Semite on account of his racial charac-
> teristics, was not fitted to live side by side with the Aryan Christian.
> *(An Outline of Jewish History,* Vol. iii, p. 316.)

But Zionism was not the only reaction to these developments.

The masses of working-class Jews, especially in Russia, responded rather by joining the revolutionary movement and coming into irreconcilable conflict with Zionism.

Zionist Ideology

Political Zionism is a reactionary bourgeois-nationalist ideology based on two fundamental fallacies: (1) that the Jews throughout the world constitute a nation, and (2) that anti-Semitism is incurable and eternal.

That the Jews on a world scale, lacking a common territory, language, cultural and economic life, do not constitute a nation in any generally recognized (let alone Marxist) sense of the term hardly needs to be demonstrated. Zionism, however, looks upon the Jews as a nation only in a biological sense: that they are presumed to be the literal descendants of the Jews of ancient times; and in a spiritual sense: that they possess a common background (as some put it, the "same historic memory"), a common religion and, arising from this, the elements of a common culture. Indeed, Zionism sees the Jews as set apart by mystical bonds which non-Jews are incapable of understanding or sharing. Jacob Neusner, Professor of Religious Studies at Brown University, expresses it in these words:

> The inwardness of Zionism—its piety and spirituality—is not to be comprehended by the world, only by the Jew, for, like the Judaism it transformed and transcended, to the world it was worldly and political, stiffnecked and stubborn . . . but to the Jew it was something other, not to be comprehended by the gentile. ("Zionism and the 'Jewish Problem,' " *Midstream,* November 1969.)

Closely connected with such ideas of innate distinctness is the concept of the Jews as a "chosen people," destined to play a unique role in history, and thereby set apart from all other peoples.

In short, Zionism asserts the existence of an unbridgeable gulf between Jew and non-Jew. In its own way it upholds the racist doctrine of the anti-Semites that Jews are inherently different from other peoples and hence incapable of becoming integrated with them.

Directly related to this is the thesis that anti-Semitism is inherent in non-Jews and hence ineradicable. Pinsker regarded anti-Semitism as biological in nature. He wrote:

> Judeophobia is a variety of demonopathy with the distinction that it is not peculiar to particular races, but is common to the whole of mankind. . . . As a psychic aberration it is hereditary, and as a disease transmitted for two thousand years it is incurable. (*Auto-Emancipation,* p. 9.)

Herzl, it is true, viewed the roots of anti-Semitism as social rather than biological. But he saw it as being none the less inevitable, since he regarded the social relationships between Jews and gentiles as essentially unchangeable. It was the Jews themselves, he maintained, who carried the seeds of anti-Semitism with them wherever they went. This idea was echoed 50 years later by Chaim Weizmann, then head of the World Zionist Organization, who said:

> I believe the one fundamental cause of anti-Semitism . . . is that the Jew exists. We seem to carry anti-Semitism in our knapsacks wherever we go. The growth and intensity of anti-Semitism is proportional to the number of Jews or to the density of Jews in a given country. (*The Jewish Case Before the Anglo-American Committee on Palestine,* p. 7.)

Herzl wrote: "Above all I recognized the emptiness and futility of efforts to 'combat' anti-Semitism." (*The Diaries of Theodor Herzl,* p. 6.) He concluded, therefore, that the solution of the Jewish question lies not in fighting to end anti-Semitism and to achieve full equality for the Jewish people in all countries where they live, but in separating Jew from non-Jew—in establishing a Jewish state in which the Jewish nation, scattered in exile for some 2,000 years, could be reunited.

To Herzl and many of his followers the location of such a Jewish state was immaterial. Herzl regarded Palestine and Argentina as equally acceptable. And he fought for the acceptance of a British offer of territory in Uganda. But to others of his followers, chiefly those from Eastern Europe, a Jewish state could only mean Palestine. Weizmann writes in his autobiography:

> Kishinev [the frightful pogrom of 1903—H. L.] had only intensified in the Jews of Russia the ineradicable longing for a Jewish home in Pal-

estine—in Palestine and not elsewhere. Elsewhere meant for them only a continuation of the old historic rounds of refuge. They wanted Palestine because that meant restoration in every sense. *(Trial and Error,* p. 92.)

For David Ben-Gurion the basis of the Jewish state in Palestine is "the Messianic vision of the redemption of the Jewish people and all mankind." This is "the soul of prophetic Jewry, in all its forms and metamorphoses until this day, and it is the secret of the open and hidden devotion of world Jewry to the State of Israel." (Address to the 25th World Zionist Congress, December 28, 1960.)

Thus political Zionism becomes joined with the older religious Zionism with its "Messianic vision" of the return to the "promised land" of the Old Testament. But it was not an ancient longing to return to Zion that gave the impulse to political Zionism; this idea had long existed only as an ossified religious ritual. "Next year in Jerusalem" was uttered yearly by innumerable Jews who had not the faintest expectation—or desire—of returning to Jerusalem at any time. That impulse was provided rather by the rise of modern anti-Semitism of which we have already spoken, originally in the late 19th century and later, in its most hideous form, in the days of Hitlerism.

Zionism as an Organized Movement

Political Zionism is not only an ideology; it is also an organized world movement. The World Zionist Organization, launched through Herzl's initiative, held its First Congress in 1897. That Congress stated: "The aim of Zionism is to create for the Jewish people a home in Eretz Israel secured by public law." The 23rd Congress, held after the establishment of the State of Israel, revised this aim as follows: "The task of Zionism is the consolidation of the State of Israel, the ingathering of the exiles in Eretz Israel and the fostering of the unity of the Jewish people." Clearly, Israel is looked upon as the homeland of *all* Jews, to which the "world Jewish nation" scattered in exile is to be returned.

Zionism regards Jews as aliens in the lands in which they live. It seeks to withdraw them from the struggles for democracy and progress in their own countries as being of no consequence to them as Jews. It strives to build a wall between Jewish and non-Jewish workers, maintaining that the only real bond of Jewish workers is that with other Jews, including Jewish capitalists. It rejects socialism as an answer to anti-Semitism and is bitterly hostile to the socialist countries, insisting that anti-Semitism, being incurable, is no less rife in these than in the capitalist countries.

It stands at the very opposite pole from the ideology of working-class internationalism, which calls for the unity of workers of all countries against their common class enemy, world monopoly capitalism, and on this basis for a common struggle against all forms of national and racial oppression as being divisive and destructive of the interests of workers everywhere. In its extreme nationalism and separatism, in its capitulation to anti-Semitism, in its efforts to divide Jewish workers from other workers, Zionism serves the interests of the exploiters and oppressors of all workers and all peoples.

2. ZIONISM AND ISRAEL

How the State of Israel Was Born

The State of Israel had its origins in the UN resolution of November 29, 1947 which partitioned Palestine into two states, one Jewish and one Arab.

It was not, as is maintained in some quarters, a creation of Britain. To be sure, British imperialism encouraged Jewish settlement in Palestine through the Balfour Declaration of 1917. But it did so only to pit Jews and Arabs against one another in order to perpetuate British rule under the League of Nations Mandate. In the later years of the Mandate the British severely restricted Jewish immigration into Palestine, and at no time did they support the formation of an independent Jewish state.

The British ruling circles, though they had surrendered the Mandate in 1947 on the grounds that internal conflict made it impossible to exercise it, opposed the partition of Palestine. Their UN representatives abstained from voting on the partition resolution and on all related questions, and they announced that Britain would do nothing to implement the resolution if either the Jews or the Arabs objected to it. What they hoped was that because of Jewish-Arab antagonisms partition would fail and that in the ensuing chaos the UN would find no alternative other than continuation of British rule in one form or another.

Furthermore, it was British imperialism which instigated the Arab states to attack the new-born State of Israel in 1948. These Arab states were at that time governed by puppet rulers subservient to Britain and their armed forces were commanded by British officers taking orders from London. The war fought by Israel in 1948 was in fact a war against British imperialism. "The objective of this military action by British imperialism," writes Bert Ramelson, "was to frustrate the implementing of the UN resolution, to hang on to the whole of Palestine, and by parcelling it out among Arab stooge rulers, to retain indirectly what Britain previously held directly as the mandatory power." *(The Middle East,* pp. 13–14.)

Nor did the Truman Administration in this country display any great enthusiasm for partition. On the contrary, motivated largely by pressures emanating from the oil interests, it maneuvered to modify or to circumvent the partition proposals.

The main initiative leading to the UN action came from the Soviet Union, supported by the other socialist countries. In a speech on May 14, 1947 Soviet UN representative Andrei Gromyko called for "the creation of a single Arab-Jewish state with equal rights for Jews and Arabs . . . as the solution most deserving attention, of this complicated problem." But should this prove unrealizable because of sharpened Jewish-Arab hostility, "then it would be necessary to consider an alternative solution which . . . consists of the division of Israel into two states—one, Jewish, and one, Arab."

Among the reasons given by Gromyko for his proposals was the need to find a haven for the many Jewish refugees who had been left stranded (thanks mainly to the refusal of the capitalist states to admit them). But he also presented a more cogent reason, namely, that there *already* existed a significant Jewish community in Palestine. He said:

> . . . We must bear in mind the incontestable fact that the population of Palestine consists of two peoples, Arabs and Jews. Each of these has

its historical roots in Palestine. That country has become the native land of both these peoples, and both of them occupy an important place in the country economically and culturally. Neither history nor the conditions which have arisen in Palestine now can justify any unilateral solution of the Palestine problem, either in favor of the creation of an independent Arab state, ignoring the lawful rights of the Jewish people, or in favor of the creation of a Jewish state, ignoring the lawful rights of the Arab population. . . . A just settlement can be found only if account is taken in sufficient degree of the lawful interests of both peoples.

In 1946 there were in Palestine some 608,000 Jews, nearly one-third of the total population of 1,973,000. These constituted a substantial and distinct Jewish community. To be sure, they were in the main recent immigrants who had come during the war. The bulk of them came, however, not as Zionist usurpers of Arab land but rather, in the face of enormous difficulties, as refugees from the horrors of Nazism, most of whom had literally nowhere else to go.

The Soviet Union has always been strongly opposed to the Zionist concept of a Jewish state. But that was not the issue here. Under the circumstances that prevailed in 1947, it would have been just as wrong to agree to complete Arab domination as to accede to the Zionist demand to make all of Palestine a Jewish homeland. The course proposed by the Soviet Union was therefore the only realistic and just one available.

Had the Jews and Arabs formed a common front against British imperialism at the end of World War II, the natural outcome of their victory in such a struggle would have been some form of binational state. In fact, it was such a possibility that the Soviet proposals envisaged. But this was not to be, and there remained in the end only the alternative of partition.

The basis for the coming into being of the State of Israel was not created by Zionism. Until the advent of Hitlerism with its monstrous crimes against the Jews, comparatively few Jews were induced by the Zionists to migrate to Palestine (in 1931 the Jewish population was about 175,000, a little more than one-fourth of the 1946 figure). It was the wave of immigration of refugees during and immediately after the war that first created a substantial Jewish community, and the new wave of immigration from Eastern Europe after 1948, stemming from the horrors of Hitlerism, that swelled the size of this community, doubling its numbers within a few years. But it was the Zionists who retained control and who fashioned the state according to their own design.

The validity of Israel's existence as a state derives from the UN partition resolution. However, the state envisioned by that resolution is not that conceived of and established by Zionism.

For Jews Exclusively

The Jewish state envisioned by Zionism was to be *exclusively* Jewish, for only in such a state, according to Zionist doctrine, would it be possible to escape anti-Semitism. That Palestine was also populated by Arabs was either ignored or regarded as an inconvenience to be removed or at best tolerated.

Herzl spoke of settlement in Palestine in terms of "a people without a land to a land without a people." For him the Palestinian Arabs simply did not exist as a people. And this attitude has continued to prevail up to the present time.

It was manifested in pronounced form by David Ben-Gurion, of whom the Israeli writer Aubrey Hodes says:

> Ben-Gurion had little time for the Arabs. . . . He despised the Arab way of life and warned publicly against the danger that Israel would become another Levantine country "like Saudi Arabia or Iraq." . . . It is significant that during his thirteen years as Prime Minister of Israel he did not pay a single official visit to the city of Nazareth, the largest Arab center in Israel. (*Dialogue With Ishmael*, p. 67.)

Michael Bar-Zohar, Ben-Gurion's biographer, gives the following picture of the latter's views at the time of the 1948 war:

> Ben-Gurion remained skeptical about any possibility of coexistence with the Arabs. The fewer there were living within the frontiers of the new Jewish state, the better he would like it. . . . (While this might be called racialism, the whole Zionist movement actually was based on the principle of a purely Jewish community in Palestine. When the various Zionist institutions appealed to the Arabs not to leave the Jewish state but to become an integral part of it, they were being hypocritical to some extent.) (*Ben-Gurion*, p. 103.)

Indeed, many were not thus hypocritical; they made no bones about wanting the Arabs out. The idea that Arabs do not really count as people remains widely prevalent in Israel today, as noted by another Israeli writer, Amos Oz, in these words:

In time, Naomi Shemer [in her hit song "Jerusalem of Gold"] was to express this state of mind by describing East Jerusalem in terms of: "—the market place is empty/ And none goes down to the Dead Sea/ By way of Jericho"—meaning, of course: The market place is empty *of Jews* and no *Jew* goes down to the Dead Sea by way of Jericho. A remarkable revelation of a remarkably characteristic way of thinking. ("Meaning of Homeland," *New Outlook,* December 1967.)

In keeping with the Zionist concept, the establishment of Jewish settlements was from the outset based on displacement of Arabs by Jews. Uri Avnery, member of the Knesset and editor of the Israeli weekly *Ha'olam Hazeh,* writes in his book *Israel Without Zionists* of Hebrew Labor, Hebrew Land and Hebrew Defense as the three main themes of Zionism. He says:

. . . Hebrew Labor meant, necessarily, no Arab Labor. The "redemption of the land" often meant, necessarily, "redeeming" it from the Arab *fellahin* who happened to be living on it. A Jewish plantation owner who employed Arabs in his orange grove was a traitor to the cause, a despicable reactionary who not only deprived a Jewish worker of work, but even more important, deprived the country of a Jewish worker. His grove had to be picketed, the Arabs had to be evicted by force. . . . This was the battle of Hebrew Labor, which continued for two generations, and relapses of which still trouble present-day Israel from time to time. . . .

The struggle for the redemption of the land became, at times, as violent. The land was bought, often at exorbitant prices, with good money raised mostly by poor Jews abroad. In many cases, the Arab who sold it did not live on the land, but was a rich *effendi* whiling away his life in the casinos of Beirut or the French Riviera. He had no particular care for the fate of the poor *fellahin* tenants who made their meager living there. These were simply evicted when the land was redeemed by the Jewish National Fund to set up a *kibbutz.* If some of them later attacked the *kibbutz,* it only showed that an efficient system of armed defense was imperative. Thus the *Histadrut* became the sponsor and the patron of the *Haganah,* the underground army based on the *kibbutzim,* which became the forerunner of today's Israel Defense Army (p. 85).

There were some, notable among them the father of "spiritual Zionism," Ahad Ha'am, who spoke out strongly against such an approach to the Arabs, regarding it as a serious blunder. But this was no "mistake"; the fact is that such a racist attitude toward Arabs is inherent in Zionism.

Israeli Arabs: Second-Class Citizens

In accord with the Zionist concept, Israel has been established as a state in which any Jew anywhere in the world may claim citizenship and enjoy special ethnic and religious privileges. Until recently such citizenship had to be claimed by migrating to Israel, but now even this is not necessary. An amendment to the Israeli citizenship law, passed in May 1971, permits any Jew who "expresses a desire to settle in Israel" to become a citizen without budging one inch.*

On the other hand, Arabs whose ancestors have lived there for countless generations are merely tolerated as aliens, reduced to second-class citizenship and treated as a "fifth column" whose sympathies lie with Israel's enemies.

From the beginning, Israeli Arabs have been subjected to the emergency military regulations imposed by the British in 1945 on both Jews and Arabs in Palestine. With the founding of the State of Israel these regulations ceased to be applied to Jews but continued to be imposed on Arabs. Until very recently, Arabs were required to obtain military passes to travel from one part of the country to another. And under these regulations areas of land were closed off for "security" reasons and their inhabitants were forbidden to enter them. Through this device nearly half the land belonging to Israeli Arabs has been taken from them and turned over to kibbutzim. Many have been converted into "internal refugees," living in shacks in nearby villages and seeking work as agricultural laborers. Others have found their way into the cities and into already overcrowded

* The chief motivation behind the amendment is the current drive to bring Soviet Jews to Israel, of which we shall have more to say later. By permitting Jews living in the Soviet Union to be granted Israeli citizenship, it becomes possible, at least for propaganda purposes, to charge that "Israeli citizens" are being prohibited by the Soviet government from going to their homeland.

slum ghettos, where they are often forced to live in condemned houses which have more than once collapsed, killing or seriously injuring their inhabitants.

According to official statistics, annual earnings of non-Jewish families in 1967 were less than 64 per cent of those of Jewish families, and this with 1.6 earners per family compared to 1.3 in Jewish families. (One looks in vain in the official statistics for data on Israeli Arabs as such.)

Only half of the Arab workers are members of Histradrut (the trade union organization) as against three-fourths of the Jewish workers. Only one-third are members of the Health Insurance Fund (Kupat Cholim) as against 72 per cent of Jewish workers. Moreover, the Fund has few clinics in Arab villages, so that the Arab members receive much poorer service than the Jewish.

In institutions of higher learning Arabs are only 1.5 per cent of the student body, though they are 12 per cent of the population. And from certain fields of study they are excluded altogether as "security risks."

Arab farmers are discriminated against with regard to credits, irrigation, mechanization and other forms of government assistance. Most Arab villages lack labor councils or labor exchanges through which unemployed workers can seek work under union conditions, while these Histadrut institutions are the rule in Jewish communities.

No Arabs have occupied top level positions in government and the number in middle ranks has been insignificant. Only in 1971 was an Arab appointed, for the first time, to a minor cabinet post.

Illustrative of the whole pattern of discrimination is the city of Nazareth. Lower Nazareth, the old city dating back to Biblical times, has a population of some 30,000, all Arab. Upper Nazareth, located on the surrounding hills, with 22,000 residents, consists mostly of Jewish settlers. Lower Nazareth has almost no industry and many of its workers are forced to seek employment in other cities. On the other hand, Upper Nazareth boasts a Dodge assembly plant, a large textile mill and a number of other modern factories. In these factories few Arabs are employed, and these largely as janitors. Upper Nazareth also boasts a beautiful Histadrut vacation resort—for Jews only. The only Arabs there at the time I visited it in

1970 were two who were employed in the kitchen. Nor are Arabs able to rent apartments in the new apartment houses of Upper Nazareth.

I also encountered the "internal refugees" in Nazareth. On the outskirts of the city I came across a collection of galvanized iron shacks. These, I learned, were inhabited by the former population of the nearby village of Ma'lul, from which they had been expelled by the Israeli authorities not long after the 1948 war. I learned also that nearly one-third of the Arab residents of Nazareth are refugees from nearby villages. And these in turn are only part of a much larger body of such "internal refugees"—Arabs deprived of their homes and lands because they may have been temporarily absent from them during or immediately after the war, or for reasons of "security."

This situation was recently brought dramatically to a head by the former Arab residents of the towns of Biram and Iqrit, from which they had been expelled in 1948 on "security" grounds. At the time, they were told they would be permitted to return after a few weeks, but the promise was never honored and most of the property was turned over to Jewish settlements and kibbutzim—as *abandoned property!*

When, in early 1972, the military bars were lifted in the area, these expelled villagers, who had been living as refugees within Israel all these years, sought to return to what remained of their lands. They were refused and were beaten up by border guard policemen when they tried to enter them. The affair stirred up intense public feeling and led to unprecedented mass demonstrations in support of the villagers. But the Meir government was adamant. "Security" came first, the rights of Israeli Arabs second.

In all aspects of life, Israeli Arabs suffer severe discrimination and are treated like outsiders in their own country. And those who have been made refugees are not permitted to return to their homeland.

During the 1948 war some 750,000 Arabs either fled in panic or were driven from their homes, to become refugees living in wretched settlements of tents and shacks in the surrounding Arab countries, mainly in Jordan. As a result, cities and towns once wholly populated by Arabs are now either entirely Jewish or have small Arab minorities. Thus the formerly all-Arab city of Jaffa now has only 6,000 Arabs and formerly all-Arab towns like Beersheba and Ashkelon have none. The Israeli rulers seized more than half the territory allotted to the Palestinian Arab state in the UN partition resolution of 1947, and they proceeded to take over the property abandoned by the Arabs who had fled. Don Peretz writes in his book *Israel and the Palestine Arabs:*

> Abandoned property was one of the greatest contributions toward making Israel a viable state. . . . Of the 370 Jewish settlements established between 1948 and the beginning of 1953, 350 were on absentee property. . . . In 1954 more than one-third of Israel's Jewish population lived on absentee property and nearly a third of the new immigrants (250,000 people) settled in urban areas abandoned by Arabs. . . . Ten thousand shops, businesses and stores were left in Jewish hands. At the end of the Mandate, citrus holdings in the area of Israel totalled about 240,000 dunams, of which half were Arab-owned. Most of the Arab groves were taken over by the Israeli Custodian of Absentee Property (pp. 143, 165).

And despite a repeatedly reaffirmed UN resolution calling for either repatriation or compensation of the refugees, the Israeli authorities have rejected all responsibility for the refugees. Behind this policy lies the idea that the fewer Arabs remaining in Israel the better.*

* The only group in Israel which has waged a consistent, uncompromising struggle against anti-Arab oppression and for Jewish-Arab unity has been the Communist Party of Israel, headed by Meir Vilner and Tawfiq Toubi. There have been, it is true, others who opposed the prevailing Zionist approach to the Arabs and who called for Jewish-Arab unity. The Ihud (Union) Movement for Jewish-Arab Rapprochement, headed by Dr. Judah L. Magnes and including among its leading figures the noted philosopher Martin Buber, called during the thirties and forties for bringing Jews and Arabs together and for a binational state in Palestine. But its approach, based on idealistic appeals to both sides and not on opposition to the chauvinistic Zionist doctrines, attracted few followers. At the time of Dr. Magnes' death in 1948 it was still a tiny minority and after that it folded up altogether. The Hashomer Hatzair Workers' Party, predecessor of the present Mapam, also called for a binational state. But this, too, represented only a small minority. Moreover, Mapam, like the other Zionist parties, opposed the ending of the British mandate and the establishment of an independent state until the Jews should become a majority of the population. Today there are groupings which purport to seek Jewish-Arab unity, but these, too, operate fully within the Zionist orbit and are, to say the least, ineffectual. The support of Israeli Arabs goes largely to the Communist Party, which in recent elections has received between 30 and 40 per cent of the Arab vote.

Oriental Jews: An Oppressed Majority

Discrimination in Israel is not confined to Arabs. It is visited also on the darker-skinned Sephardic or Oriental Jews, coming mainly from Arab countries such as Yemen, Iraq and the North African states, and now comprising about 60 per cent of Israel's population. Much poorer and less educated than Jews of Western origin, these have been thrust down to the lowest rungs of the economic and social ladders. The recent demonstrations of the Israeli group calling itself the Black Panthers have forcefully brought their plight to public attention.

They are crowded into the most unskilled, lowest-paying jobs. According to a 1969 survey by Israel's Central Bureau of Statistics, in 1967 their average per capita yearly income was only 38.5 per cent of that of Western Jews and 42.6 per cent of that of Israeli-born Jews. In addition, they are packed into "old city" slum ghettos, with a housing density three to five times that of other groups.

They lag far behind in education. Whereas about 60 per cent of all children entering primary school are Sephardic, at the secondary school level the proportion falls to 25 per cent and at the university level to 10 per cent.

They are victims of discrimination and prejudice and are subjected to all sorts of insults and indignities. Robert Silverberg writes:

. . . The Orientals are generally swarthy or dark-skinned. To a European Jew they look very much like Arabs, and the treatment accorded them is not very sympathetic. As the American anthropologist Raphael Patai . . . expressed it in his book *Israel Between East and West,* "In addition to instability, emotionalism, impulsiveness, unreliability, and incompetence, the Oriental Jew is accused [by European-born Israelis] of habitual lying and cheating, laziness, uncontrolled temper, superstitiousness, childishness, lack of cleanliness and in general, 'primitivity' and 'lack of culture.' " (*If I Forget Thee O Jerusalem,* p. 480.)

" 'Cushi,' the Biblical term for Negro," according to *The New York Times* (January 29, 1965), "has taken on the same pejorative meaning in Israel as 'nigger' in the United States."

Illustrative of the attitude toward "Orientals" is an article by Yael Dayan, daughter of Moshe Dayan and a well-known novelist, in the Israeli newspaper *Yediot Aharonot* (March 22, 1968). She writes about her difficulties in selling a house. "It's the neighborhood," the real estate agents tells her. She explains:

> The house's only neighbors are "Orientals." It borders on a Yemenite quarter called Morashah, and actually forms the borderline between the respectable neighborhood of Naveh Magen, which boasts of Israeli army commanders, and the Yemenite quarter, with one-story houses and nice gardens whose sons serve in the army. . . . It was thus that ghettos were formed. Thus grew the Negro, the Puerto Rican and the Jewish slums. Would you want your daughter to marry a Negro? Would you want to have a Jew as your neighbor? . . .
>
> I don't know which is more insulting—the fact that the whole phenomenon exists, or the total lack of shame implicit in openly admitting it. "I would have paid 5,000 more for the house had it been in another neighborhood," a respectable lady told me. Five thousand Israeli pounds more so that Rabinovitz's children won't play with the children of this quarter. Five thousand pounds more so that they won't mix, God forbid, with those who have dark eyes and black hair.

Oriental Jews are grossly under-represented in the Israeli government. Of 120 seats in the Knesset, they occupy only some 20-odd. In the Israeli Cabinet they hold only the Ministry of Posts and the Ministry of Police. And even this minimal representation is meaningless, since these officials were designated by the dominant Labor Party and other parties completely controlled by Western Jews, primarily to provide a fig leaf for their policy of discrimination.

The fact is that Israel has been ruled since its birth by a group of Zionists mainly of Eastern European origin, to whom a "Jewish state" and "Jewishness" mean a state based on the culture of Eastern European Jewry. Nissim Rejwan, a prominent Oriental Jewish writer, says:

> When Israel's present East European Zionist Establishment and its spokesmen talk of the absolute necessity of preserving the country's Jewishness what they in fact have in mind is little more than *their own brand* of Jewish culture. For them, this now thoroughly secularized culture of the Jews of the Pale of Settlement represents "Jewishness" pure and simple. ("Israel as an Open Society," *The Jewish Spectator*, December 1967.)

Correspondingly, the culture of the Middle Eastern Jews is rejected as not being "Jewish," and the dominant group of Western origin, though now decidedly in the minority, nevertheless seeks to impose its culture on a majority whose cultural traditions are quite different.

Underlying this is the Zionist conception of Israel as a "Western" society which is Middle Eastern only geographically. The Zionists' greatest fear is that Israel will become "Levantinized." And what greater source of such a danger is there than the already "Levantinized" Oriental Jews who are a majority of the population, not to speak of the added 12 per cent of the population which is Arab? Accordingly, every effort is made to downgrade and smother their culture—to "Westernize" them, to teach their children "Western" ways in the schools and to relegate them to a subordinate place in Israeli society. And every effort is made to promote immigration of Western Jews in order to offset the majority status of the Oriental Jews.

A Theocratic State

Finally, the Jewish state of the Zionists is a theocratic state in which Orthodox Judaism occupies a privileged position. Not even Conservative or Reform Judaism has any recognized standing. This is a natural outgrowth of Zionist ideology, which regards Judaism as central among the distinguishing features of the Jewish people, as that feature which confers upon them the special status of a "chosen people." And this means *Orthodox* Judaism, whose doctrines and practices have been built into the life of the country.

A Jew is defined according to the Halakic code of Orthodox Judaism as one who is born of a Jewish mother or is converted to Judaism in accordance with the rigorous Orthodox procedures. And only recently this definition was reaffirmed by the Knesset, which overruled a decision of the Israeli Supreme Court abolishing it and defining a Jew as anyone who declared oneself as such.

A separate group of religious schools is maintained at government expense within the framework of the public school system, for the benefit of the religious parties. These parties, though commanding no more than 15 per cent of the vote, are able to exercise a power far beyond their numbers, since the dominant Labor Party and its predecessor, Mapai, have counted on coalition with them to provide a majority in the Knesset and have in turn acquiesced to their policies for this reason as well as on ideological grounds.

Consequently, there is to this day no such thing as civil marriage or divorce in Israel. A Jew can marry a non-Jew only by going out of the country to do so. And there are numerous other such religious restrictions to which all Israeli citizens are subjected.

I. F. Stone writes: " 'It's Hard to be a Jew' was the title of Sholem Aleichem's most famous story." But in Israel, he notes, it's hard to be a non-Jew, and especially an Arab non-Jew. ("Holy War," *The New York Review of Books,* August 3, 1967.)

Such is the Zionist conception of a Jewish state. It is a racist conception, based on the fallacy that freedom from one's own oppression can be attained by oppressing others. And it has made of Israel a country permeated by narrow Jewish nationalism and chauvinism. Small wonder that it arouses such intense hostility among Arabs.

3. "SOCIALIST" ZIONISM

"Socialist" Trends: Anti-Marxist and "Marxist"

Almost from the very inception of the Zionist movement there emerged within it trends seeking to unite the idea of Zionism with that of socialism. As early as 1900 one such trend began to take organized form as the Poale Zion (Workers of Zion), whose first groups appeared in tsarist Russia. These varied greatly in their ideological positions, but there soon crystallized a movement based on the concept of a socialist Jewish state in Palestine. In 1905 a Poale Zion Party was formed in the United States, in the city of Baltimore, which stated in its declaration of principles:

Since the development of mankind expresses itself through the development of individual nations, since the normal socio-economic, political and cultural development of every people requires a majority status in some land, and since such a development can only be realized in the historical homeland of a given people, we attest our belief in Zionism which strives for an openly secured homeland for the Jewish people in Palestine.

Since we consider a society based on private ownership as a society in which a minority owns the means of production and lives on the labor of the majority, we will strive to alter unjust forms and to introduce a socialist society. . . .
We want the future Jewish state to be established insofar as possible on socialist principles. . . . *(Yiddisher Kemfer* 1906. Quoted by Nachman Syrkin, "Beginnings of Socialist Zionism," in Gendzier, *A Middle East Reader,* p. 112.)

The leading ideologist of this trend, which took an openly anti-Marxist direction, was Nachman Syrkin (1868–1924). On the other hand there arose a trend, led by Ber Borochov (1881–1917), which sought to merge Zionism with Marxism. Borochov wrote:

. . . the class struggle can take place only where the worker toils, *i.e.,* where he has already occupied a certain workplace. The weaker his status at this position, the less ground he has for a systematic struggle. As long as the worker does not occupy a definite position, he can wage no struggle. It is therefore in his own interests to protect his position.
From whatever angle we may approach the national question to determine the scope of its existence for the proletariat . . . we must always arrive finally at its material basis, *i.e.,* at the question of the place of employment and the strategic base of struggle which the territory represents for the proletariat. ("The National Question and the Class Struggle," in Hertzberg, *The Zionist Idea,* p. 368.)

Jewish workers, said Borochov, are removed from the basic branches of industry; they are at the periphery of production. This renders their economic life stagnant, their culture at a low ebb and their political life insecure. *(Selected Essays in Socialist-Zionism.)* Hence, lacking its own territorial base the Jewish working class cannot carry on the class struggle under normal conditions. Only within the framework of a Jewish state can it normalize the conditions of struggle and successfully pursue the fight for socialism. Moreover, as an oppressed group, Jewish workers can achieve their liberation only through their own activity. They cannot rely, writes Daniel Ben Nachum, "on external forces: on general revolutionary changes that would bring salvation to them, too, although of necessity their part in these changes would be only limited and marginal." ("The Abiding and Transitory Elements in Borochovism," *Israel Horizons,* March 1971.) And this, again, means that they must have their own territorial base.

Both varieties of "socialist" Zionism—the anti-Marxist and the pseudo-Marxist—find expression today, in this country as well as in Israel. Among the Zionist organizations in the United States is Poale Zion—United Labor Zionist Organization of America— whose statement of purposes includes the building of Israel as a "cooperative commonwealth." In Israel the dominant Labor Party professes to be socialist and is affiliated with the Socialist International. The United Workers Party (Mapam) has since 1948 had among its purposes "the creation of a classless society" and has professed an adherence to Marxism. Its affiliate in this country, Americans for Progressive Israel-Hashomer Hatzair, describes its program as "Socialist-Zionist."

But all these organizations and parties are firmly wedded to Zionist separatism—to a nationalism which is totally incompatible with the proletarian internationalism that forms the cornerstone of genuine Marxism. Despite its claims to be Marxist, Borochovism tends, no less than any other variant of Zionism, to isolate the Jewish workers from the rest of the working class in their own countries instead of uniting them against their common exploiters.

Illustrative of this approach is a declaration issued by the Russian Poale Zion in the midst of the revolutionary upheaval in 1905. It states:

> Since we do not expect from the revolution any radical solution of the Jewish question and since we have a separate historic mission, we cannot occupy ourselves with the preparatory work for the revolution. . . . We Jews come forward as an independent social group only where it is a question of defending specific Jewish interests. (*The Jewish Worker*, Moscow, 1925, Vol. II, p. 401; quoted in Magil, *Israel in Crisis*, p. 124.)

Thus did these "socialists" preach abandonment of the struggle, in the face of the fact that the future of the Russian Jewish workers clearly lay in uniting with the workers of all other nationalities for the overthrow of the brutally oppressive, pogromist tsarist regime. Today, too, their successors manifest a concern about socialism not in their own countries, but only in Israel.

The claim of these elements to speak as Marxists is patently fraudulent. Hence it is not surprising that they have been repudiated by the world socialist movement, from the early days of Zionism up to the present. The noted British Marxist R. Palme Dutt writes:

> When the Zionist movement, alongside its close ties with the money-bags, sought also to develop sections which called themselves "socialist" and applied on this basis to the old Socialist International, the International Socialist Bureau, representing at that time all sections of the socialist movement from the Fabians to the Bolsheviks, turned them down. ("The Middle East—Explosion or Solution?," *Labour Monthly,* February 1970.)

And in 1920, when a majority at the Fifth World Congress of Poale Zion voted to join the Communist International, its application was flatly rejected. Today the Israeli Labor Party is affiliated with the so-called Socialist International and participates actively in its congresses, but this body is no more "socialist" than is the Israeli Labor Party.

"Socialism" in Israel

The "socialist" Zionists maintain that Israel, in keeping with their ideas, has developed as a socialist country. Shlomo Avneri, Chairman of the Department of Political Science at Hebrew University in Jerusalem, contends that Zionist policy "resulted in a *conscious* creation of a Jewish peasantry and a Jewish working class. . . ." He adds:

> It was the same conceptual framework which placed the kibbutzim and moshavim in such socially strategic positions in Israel society, created the Histadrut not as a mere trade union organization but as a Society of Laborers (Hevrat Ovdim), owning industries, banks and cooperatives and trying to coordinate a vision of social reconstruction with political aims and manipulation.
> In other words, Socialism and Zionism became inseparable. The socialistically-oriented structure became pivotal to the establishment of a Jewish society. ("The Sources of Israeli Socialism," *Israel Horizons,* March 1971.)

He concludes that "the commanding heights of the Israeli economy are very much under public control." Others, on the grounds that a major share of Israeli enterprises—agricultural, industrial, financial and commercial—are cooperatively or publicly owned, assert that Israel is essentially socialist or is definitely moving toward socialism.

But this is confusing form with substance. The existence of public and cooperative sectors of the economy, however extensive, does not in itself mean the existence of socialism. A socialist society is one in which political power is in the hands of the working class and its allies, in which the exploitation of wage labor for private profit has been effectively abolished, and in which production is planned and is designed to serve the needs of the people. In Israel none of these features is present, as even a limited examination will show.

Let us look at the public sector. As of 1960, according to a study by Chaim Barkai, it accounted for 21.1 per cent of the net domestic product.* This includes enterprises owned by the central government, local governments and Zionist institutions, chiefly the Jewish Agency, which is involved in virtually every branch of the economy.† What is the nature of the government investment? Chaim Bermont describes it as follows:

> The government itself is a heavy investor, not for doctrinal reasons, but because of the paucity of private capital and the non-commercial nature of many of the projects which the government is anxious to promote. In general, public money goes where private enterprise and the Histadrut fear to tread, like the Timna Copper Mines. Where the government can find a private buyer for its holdings, it will dispose of them. Thus Israel has in recent years witnessed a process of denationalization, and the Haifa oil refineries, 65 per cent of the stock of Palestine Potash (which owns the Dead Sea works) and numerous public assets, have been sold to private buyers. (*Israel*, p. 166.)

Thus, government investment is limited to operations of a state capitalist character and is no more "socialist" than, say, government ownership of oil- and steel-producing facilities in Brazil. Moreover, the trend is clearly toward reducing government holdings, not ex-

---

* Chaim Barkai, "The Public, Histadrut, and Private Sectors in the Israeli Economy," *Sixth Report 1961–1963* (Jerusalem: Falk Project, 1964), p. 26. Cited by Halevi and Klinov-Malul, *The Economic Development of Israel*, p. 113.

† We shall have more to say about the role of the Jewish Agency in a later chapter.

panding them. Since 1967 this process has accelerated, and to Bermont's list may be added such enterprises as the ZIM steamship
line and the Timna Copper Mines. And the lion's share of these assets has been sold to *foreign* capital—an aspect which will be dealt
with below.

Then there is the Histradut sector of the economy which, according to Barkai, accounted for 20.4 per cent of the net domestic product in 1960.

In the field of agriculture this includes first of all the kibbutzim,
communal enterprises whose members, in return for their labor, are
provided with the necessities of life and receive little or no monetary remuneration. The kibbutzim have been held forth as Israel's
most shining example of socialist development. But their membership embraces less than five per cent of Israel's population. Moreover, operating as they do within the larger framework of capitalist
production, they are not immune from the economic afflictions
characteristic of agriculture under capitalism. Their agricultural
earnings are in the main not sufficient to sustain them and they are
in part dependent on regular subsidies from the Jewish Agency.

In addition, to augment the income from agriculture, the kibbutzim have turned increasingly to the establishment of factories
operated mainly with wage labor brought in from outside. The income from manufacturing is today at least equal to that from agriculture. Thus, more and more the kibbutzim are themselves becoming exploiters of wage labor. According to Ya'acov Goldschmidt,
director of an inter-kibbutz advisory unit in Tel Aviv, "The kibbutz
is a capitalist enterprise. Each enterprise must be large-scale. We
have to get the most per unit of labor. We have to get the most for
the capital invested." *(The New York Times,* November 21, 1971.)

The Histadrut sector also includes the moshavim, agricultural
settlements in which each family farms its own plot of land, with
cooperative marketing and purchasing. These are of relatively little
significance as an economic factor. Their only claim to being "socialist" is that they do not employ wage labor.

A much more important part of the Histadrut sector is the complex of industrial, commercial and financial enterprises owned by
the Hevrat Ovdim. The executive body of Histadrut is also the governing body of Hevrat Ovdim, and each member of the former is

nominally the owner of a "share" in the latter, though he receives directly no share in its income. The Histadrut is presently the largest single employer in Israel, at the same time that it purports to represent the interests of the workers in its employ. Furthermore, a large and growing share of the stock in the Hevrat Ovdim enterprises is now privately owned, a significant part of it by foreign capital.

Finally, the Histadrut sector also includes a number of producer cooperatives. In the sector as a whole the boundaries between cooperative and private ownership and control are, to put it charitably, at best fuzzy. On this point Halevi and Klinov-Malul state:

> The four parts of the sector are not equally subject to central Histadrut control, and there is a wide range of motives among the various enterprises. Nevertheless there are grounds for separating the Histadrut from the private sector: in undertaking an activity, Histadrut enterprises retain the idea that they are supposed to serve a national or class interest. The Histadrut sector therefore holds a position somewhere between the public and private sectors *(op. cit.,* p. 46).

But even if we grant the validity of this conclusion, the fact remains that the *major* share of the net domestic product is accounted for by the private sector—according to Barkai's figures 58.5 per cent. And undoubtedly the proportion is substantially higher today than it was in 1960, thanks to the growing inroads of private capital into the other sectors. In addition, the private holdings are increasingly in the hands of foreign monopoly capital, as will be shown in a later chapter.

The simple fact is that Israel is a *capitalist* country, whose economy is predominantly in the hands of a capitalist class and whose government actively and energetically courts growing investment by foreign capital. It is marked by a sharp class struggle, with the workers engaging in frequent and at times bitter strikes—ironically, most often against the Histadrut itself. It is marked by oppression and super-exploitation of Israeli Arabs and Oriental Jews. And it is marked by the maintenance of ties not with the socialist world but with the imperialist powers—with the chief enemies of socialism.

If socialism is truly to be established in Israel, this will come about only through the struggles of a united Israeli working class —Jew and Arab—against both the Israeli capitalist class and the foreign monopolies which dominate the economy. To be successful, these struggles will require unity with the workers and peasants of the Arab countries and with the world working-class movement, particularly with the socialist countries.

To all this a prime obstacle is the influence of Zionist ideology among Israeli workers. Hence to fight for socialism is to fight against Zionism.

II

IN THE SERVICE OF IMPERIALISM

1. ZIONISM'S QUEST FOR IMPERIALIST SUPPORT

The Roles of Herzl and Weizmann

Clearly, the establishment of an exclusively Jewish state, in the heart of a territory already populated by Arabs, could be pursued only at the expense of and in opposition to the Arab people, and only in league with their oppressors. Indeed, from the very outset the Zionists based their hopes of success on the support of one or another imperialist power, offering in return a Jewish state which would serve imperialist interests in the Middle East.

It is well known that Herzl sought the backing of the rulers of tsarist Russia, France, Germany and Turkey. He even tried to sell his idea to the pogromist Russian Minister of the Interior von Plehve, whose hands still dripped with blood from the slaughter of Jews in Kishinev, as an antidote to the mounting revolutionary movement in Russia.

In *The Jewish State* he wrote: "Supposing His Majesty the Sultan were to give us Palestine, we could in return undertake to regulate the whole finances of Turkey. We should there form an outpost of civilization as opposed to barbarism" (p. 30). The barbarism he referred to was the rising tide of Arab revolt against the brutal Turkish rule. Max Nordau, one of the top Zionist leaders, spelled this out in his speech at the 7th World Zionist Congress in 1905. He said:

The movement which has taken hold of a great part of the Arab people may easily take a direction which may cause harm in Palestine. . . . The Turkish government may feel itself compelled to defend its reign in Palestine, in Syria, against its subjects by armed power. . . . In such a position, Turkey might become convinced that it may be important for her to have, in Palestine and Syria, a strong and well organized people which, with all respect to the rights of the people living there, will resist any attack on the authority of the Sultan and defend this authority with all its might.

Later, during World War I, Weizmann similarly made overtures to British imperialism. In a letter to C. P. Scott, editor of the *Manchester Guardian,* written in November 1914, he stated that

we can reasonably say that should Palestine fall within the British sphere of influence, and should Britain encourage a Jewish settlement there, as a British dependency, we could have in twenty to thirty years a million Jews out there, perhaps more; they would develop the country, bring back civilization to it and form a very effective guard for the Suez Canal. *(Trial and Error,* p. 149.)

This idea was repeatedly stressed during Weizmann's efforts, which culminated in the Balfour Declaration in 1917.

It is important to note that Weizmann conceived of the Jewish settlement not as an independent state but as a dependency of Britain—of a "benevolent imperialism." He wrote:

What we wanted was . . . a British Protectorate. Jews all over the world trusted England. They knew that law and order would be established by British rule, and that under it Jewish colonizing activities and cultural development would not be interfered with. We could therefore look forward to a time when we would be strong enough to claim a measure of self-government *(ibid.,* p. 191).

Herzl had similarly conceived of the Jewish state in Palestine as a subject state under Turkish rule. The reason for this is obvious: the Jews would continue for a considerable length of time to be a minority in Palestine, hence the protection of a ruling power was needed for the establishment of a steadily growing Jewish settlement in the face of the opposition of the Arab majority.

The Goal: All of Palestine

Moreover, the Jewish state which Zionism envisioned as coming ultimately into being with the aid of British imperialism was to em-

brace *all* of Palestine—more, all of the Biblical Land of Israel.*
This idea was implicit in the Balfour Declaration, issued on November 2, 1917, which states:

> His Majesty's Government view with favor the establishment in Palestine of a National Home for the Jewish People, and will use their best endeavors to facilitate the achievement of this object, it being clearly understood that nothing shall be done which may prejudice the civil and religious rights of the non-Jewish communities in Palestine or the rights and political status enjoyed by Jews in any other country.

Note that the Declaration speaks of "civil and religious rights" of the non-Jewish communities but says nothing of *national* rights. That is, these are treated as communities *within* a Jewish National Home.

That this is how it was understood at the time was made clear by David Lloyd George in his memoirs, in which he writes that "it was contemplated that when the time arrived for according representative institutions to Palestine, if the Jews had responded to the opportunity afforded them and had become a definite majority of the inhabitants, then Palestine would become a Jewish Commonwealth." (Cited in *Trial and Error*, p. 212.) Later, when Transjordan was cut off from Palestine by the British and set up as a separate state, Weizmann and other Zionist leaders were greatly disturbed at the removal of this area from the orbit of Jewish settlement.

Within the Zionist movement, as time went on, the idea of a Jewish state embracing all of Palestine was pressed with increasing insistence. In the United States, in May 1942, a conference called by the American Emergency Committee for Zionist Affairs adopted what came to be known as the Biltmore Program, which demanded "that Palestine be established as a Jewish Commonwealth." The 1944 convention of the Zionist Organization of America also

---

* The territory included in "Eretz Yisrael"—the Biblical Land of Israel—is variously defined. In the account of God's Covenant with Abraham (Genesis, Chapters 15–17) God says: "Unto thy seed I have given this land, from the river of Egypt unto the great river, the river Euphrates. . . ." This claim the ancient Hebrews never made good. What is today referred to is rather the territory of Palestine as initially defined in the British Mandate, including Transjordan. Currently, the reference is primarily to the occupied territories, whose retention the Israeli ruling class seeks to justify. (See map, p. 6.)

adopted a resolution calling for a Jewish Commonwealth which "shall embrace the whole of Palestine, undivided and undiminished." The same stand was adopted by the World Zionist Conference held in London in 1945. If subsequently the Zionists agreed to partition of Palestine as called for by the 1947 UN resolution, this was motivated purely by expediency, with the anticipation that eventually the Jewish state *would* embrace all of Palestine.

That this is in fact the Zionist outlook has been repeatedly indicated. Thus, in the words of Yigal Allon, currently Deputy Prime Minister of Israel: "Our duty to populate 'Greater Israel' is no less important than in the past, when it was a mandate to populate the valley of the Jordan and the valley of Beisan; he who doubts this truth doubts the entire Zionist conception." (*Jerusalem Post*, April 18, 1968.)

More recently, the 28th World Zionist Congress, in January 1972, adopted a resolution stating: "Congress declares that the right of the Jewish people to Eretz Yisrael is inalienable." And the Israeli Knesset itself has endorsed this position. A resolution adopted on March 16, 1972 asserts: "The Knesset states that the historical right of the Jewish people to Eretz Yisrael is indisputable." These claims to all of Palestine (and more) violate the national rights of the Palestinian Arab people. They fly in the face of the UN Charter and the basis on which the State of Israel was established by the UN.

Small wonder that the Arabs met the Balfour Declaration with extreme hostility and that they viewed it as creating a bastion of imperialism in their midst. Nor did the Zionists do anything to dispel this hostility. During the period of the Mandate (1922–1948), when confronted with the duplicity of the British imperialists and their efforts to pit Jews and Arabs against one another, they rejected any idea of allying the Jewish settlers with the Arab peasants and workers in common struggle against British oppression—an alliance which might have led to the eventual emergence of a binational state. Instead, they pursued a policy of antagonism toward the Arabs and persisted to the end in their efforts to make Palestine a Jewish state with the aid of British imperialism. Thereby they drove the Arab peasantry into the arms of the reactionary Arab ruling class, the land-owning effendis, who were for their own reasons opposed to British rule. Throughout the Mandate, Zionism served as a buffer between British imperialism and the striving of the Palestinian Arabs for their freedom from imperialist domination.

2. AN EXPANSIONIST POLICY

The Road to War: 1956 and 1967

Virtually from the very birth of the State of Israel its rulers have undeviatingly pursued a policy of aggressive expansionism in relation to the Arab states. And toward this end they have consistently based themselves on seeking the support of the imperialist powers, in return giving support to imperialist policies in the Middle East. In the relentless struggle between the oil-hungry forces of imperialism and the Arab forces of national liberation, the Israeli ruling circles have without exception placed themselves on the side of the former.

In its early years, in return for the supply of armaments by France, Israel supported French imperialism against the struggle of the Algerian people for independence, voting consistently on the side of the imperialist forces in the United Nations.

In 1956 Israel joined with Britain and France in the invasion of Egypt. To the Israeli people the Sinai invasion was presented as an act of self-defense, necessitated because (a) the border raids on Israel by the terriorist fedayeen had become intolerable and had to be stopped, and (b) Egypt, having received substantial supplies of arms from Czechoslovakia, was preparing to attack Israel. If there were simultaneous attacks by British and French forces, this was simply a happy coincidence of which Israel could take advantage.

But the facts were quite otherwise. Though they were completely concealed at the time, they have since come fully to light, particularly with the publication in 1967 of Anthony Nutting's book *No End of a Lesson*. Nutting, then Minister of State for Foreign Affairs under Anthony Eden, was privy to the whole unsavory business and resigned from his post because of his revulsion against it.

In his book he exposes the intimate details of the plot, one of the most callous in the whole sordid history of imperialism, to overthrow Nasser, who had committed the unforgivable crime of supporting the National Liberation Front in Algeria and had capped this with the even more unforgivable crime of nationalizing the Suez Canal. Nutting describes the final unfolding of the conspiracy in the following passage:

> That day the Cabinet met in full to take the fateful decision. It proved impossible to get a final conclusion at one session, and the matter was held over until the following day. But this did not prevent the dispatch to Paris of a senior Foreign Office official with further assurances to pass on to the Israelis that we were determined to see the French plan carried out and would do all that the Israelis required in the way of air strikes against Egyptian airfields to forestall the bombing of their cities.
>
> These assurances turned the scale, and on Thursday, October 25th, Eden learned that the Israelis had decided finally to play their part in the Sinai campaign. That afternoon the Cabinet came to its final, and for some at least probably unpalatable, decision. When [Selwyn] Lloyd returned to the Foreign Office from No. 10, I did not have to ask how it had gone. It showed in his face and, though he made a brave attempt to be light-hearted, I had never seen him more grim-faced and tormented with doubts.
>
> "When is it to happen?" I asked.
>
> "October 29; next Monday," Lloyd answered. "Israel will attack through Sinai that evening and the following morning we and the French will issue our ultimatum to her and Egypt to clear the Canal Zone for us to move our troops in. Egypt will presumably, refuse, and directly she does so we shall start bombing Egyptian airfields" (pp. 104–05).

As we know, the plot failed, thanks to the opposition of U.S. imperialism for its own reasons and thanks even more to the threat of the Soviet Union to enter the conflict on Egypt's side. France and England were forced to withdraw, and Israel was eventually compelled to abandon its Sinai conquest.

But its leaders did not abandon their policy of collusion with imperialism against the Arab peoples. Now they proceeded to ally themselves with the machinations of U.S. imperialism for the overthrow of the anti-imperialist governments in both the UAR and Syria, and U.S. imperialism became the Israeli government's chief backer. This was developed as a deliberate policy by Ben-Gurion in 1957. Michael Bar Zohar records:

. . . The experiences of the Sinai campaign had convinced him that without the support or at least the good wishes of the Americans he would not again be able to act boldly. Fortunately, there existed a means of drawing the United States closer to Israel—by playing on the Communist danger. So Ben-Gurion endeavored to become the Middle East champion of anti-Communism in the eyes of Washington. "I feel sure," Dulles wrote to Ben-Gurion in August 1957, "that you share our consternation over recent developments in Syria. We are studying the problem closely, and we should like to proceed to an exchange of views with your Government on this subject in the near future."

Ben-Gurion jumped at the opportunity. "The transforming of Syria into a base for international Communism is one of the most dangerous events that the free world has to face up to. . . . I should like to draw your attention to the disastrous consequences if international Communism should succeed in establishing itself in the heart of the Middle East. I believe the free world ought not to accept this situation. Everything depends on the firm and determined line taken by the United States as a leading Power in the free world. . . ." (Ben-Gurion, pp. 241–42.)

It could hardly be put more plainly. And the Ben-Gurion government proceeded at once in this direction. It greeted the Baghdad Pact and the Eisenhower Doctrine, twin instruments of U.S. imperialist domination. In 1958, when an anti-imperialist regime took power in Iraq, Israel supported the landing of U.S. and British troops in Lebanon and Jordan on the pretext that they had been asked for as protection against the threat of Iraqi attack. Here we have the beginnings of the collusion which culminated in the Israeli aggression in 1967, just as the previous collusion with British and French imperialism had led to the Sinai invasion in 1956.

This period was marked also by the establishment of close ties with the revanchist Bonn regime in West Germany. Starting with the absolution of Nazi crimes through the payment of reparations, these involved West German investments in Israel and secret arms deals between Ben-Gurion and Konrad Adenauer. These relations have in large measure been retained since then.

In 1966, following a victory of the progressive forces in Syria, the U.S.-hatched plot to overthrow the governments of the UAR and Syria was greatly stepped up. Jordanian troops were massed on the Syrian border and in September an abortive military coup took place, whose leaders fled to Jordan when it failed. And there appeared growing signs of Israel's involvement in these machinations.

In the spring of 1966 the United States sold Israel a number of Skyhawk attack bombers. This was the first time that such offensive weapons had been sold directly to Israel, and official Israeli circles rejoiced. But it became quickly evident that this was no act of magnanimity. *The New York Times* correspondent, James Feron, reported on June 11, 1966 on some conversations with Israeli officials. The following excerpt is highly instructive:

This is the way a Foreign Office official put it: The United States has come to the conclusion that it can no longer respond to every incident around the world, that it must rely on a local power—the deterrent of a friendly power—as a first line to stave off America's direct involvement.

In the Israeli view, Defense Secretary Robert S. McNamara outlined this approach last month just a few days before the Skyhawk deal was announced. In a major address in Montreal, one that attracted considerable attention in high circles here, Mr. McNamara reviewed American commitments around the world and said:

"It is the policy of the United States to encourage and achieve a more effective partnership with those nations who can, and should, share international peacekeeping responsibilities."

Israel feels that she fits this definition and the impression that has been conveyed by some Government officials is that Foreign Minister Abba Eban and Mr. McNamara conferred over Skyhawk details in the context of this concept when the Israeli diplomat was in Washington last February.

The *quid pro quo* was clear. And it became even clearer in the events that followed. Border raids from Syria and Jordan were met with acts of massive retaliation far out of proportion to these raids —acts which were strongly condemned by the UN Security Council. Of one such attack, on the village of Es Samu in Jordan, even U.S. Ambassador Arthur J. Goldberg was impelled to state that "deplorable as these preceding incidents were . . . this deliberate governmental decision must be judged as the conscious act of responsible leaders of a member state and therefore on an entirely different level from the earlier incidents. . . ." *(The New York Times,* November 20, 1966.)

The raids were accompanied by mounting threats of military invasion of Syria. There was growing talk in official circles about the need for a "new Sinai." In an Independence Day interview, the London *Jewish Chronicle* of May 19, 1967 reports, Prime Minister Levi Eshkol stated that the only deterrent available to Israel against Syria was a powerful lightning military strike—powerful enough to produce a change of heart or even a change of government in Damascus and swift enough to prevent any other countries from rallying to Syria's support. So vehement did these threats become that UN Secretary General U Thant, in a report to the Security Council on May 19, 1967, was led to state:

> Intemperate and bellicose utterances . . . are unfortunately more or less routine on both sides of the lines in the Near East. In recent weeks, however, reports emanating from Israel have attributed to some high officials in that state statements so threatening as to be particularly inflammatory in the sense that they could only heighten emotions and thereby increase tensions on the other side of the lines.

In short, a groundwork was being laid for aggressive action just as it had been in 1956.

This chain of events culminated in the actions taken by Nasser in May 1967—the removal of the UN Emergency Force troops from the Egyptian-Israeli border, the blockade of the Straits of Tiran and the mobilization of Egyptian military forces. The purpose of these actions, he declared, was to come to the aid of Syria in the event of Israeli attack. The response of the Israeli leaders was the invasion of Egypt, Jordan and Syria in the June "six-day war."

It is not possible here to present a detailed refutation of the false contention that this was a war of self-defense and not an act of deliberate aggression in pursuit of Israeli expansionism and U.S. imperialist aims. There is ample evidence that Egypt was not planning to invade Israel and that the Israeli ruling circles knew it. Some of it is summed up by Fred J. Khouri in his extensive study, *The Arab-Israeli Dilemma,* in these words:

> . . . The very competent and highly respected Israeli military intelligence was well aware that (1) Israel continued to hold a substantial military lead over the Arabs; (2) the Arab military forces were far from sufficiently trained and organized for successful offensive operations against her; and (3) in June the UAR was not seriously preparing

or planning to invade Israel, a fact which Western correspondents in Cairo readily observed and reported to their newspapers. Not only had American, as well as Israeli, intelligence been predicting before June 5 that Israel could win a war against the Arabs without great difficulty, but both the American and French governments had assured Israel that they would come to her aid if it became absolutely necessary. . . .

Furthermore, if the Israeli leaders had really believed that an invasion was imminent and Israel's survival was at stake, they could easily have precluded any Arab attack by accepting U Thant's suggestion that UNEF be allowed to take up positions in their territory. . . . By firmly and unhesitatingly rejecting U Thant's proposals, Israel indicated that she was less interested in thwarting an Egyptian attack than she was in making sure that a UN presence did not frustrate her own ability to strike at the UAR at the time of her own choosing (pp. 281–82).

More recently, Israeli spokesmen themselves have begun to admit that Israel stood in no danger of annihilation, and that the government and the military were fully aware of this. Colonel Matatyahu Peled, who had been Quartermaster-General in the Israeli army in 1967, spells it out in these words:

I am convinced that the government never heard from the General Staff that the Egyptian military threat was dangerous to Israel, or that it did not lie in the power of Israel to defeat the Egyptian army, which was exposing itself with astounding stupidity to the crushing blow of the Israeli army.* All this talk was made only a few months after the war; it had no part in the complex of considerations of those days—this talk about the horrible danger in which Israel found itself, because of its narrow frontiers. When the Israeli army mobilized its full power, which surpassed that of the Egyptians several times, there was no person possessing any sense who believed that all this force was necessary in order to "defend" ourselves from the Egyptian threat. This force was necessary for dealing the Egyptians a crushing defeat on the battlefield, and to their Russian patrons in the political field. The claim that the Egyptian force which was concentrated on our southern border was capable of threatening Israel's existence is not only an insult to the intelligence of anyone who is capable of evaluating such matters. It is first of all an insult to the Israeli army. (*Ha'aretz,* March 19, 1972.)

* Peled is referring here to the following statement in the Israel cabinet's resolution of June 4, 1967: "After hearing a report on the military and political situation from the Prime Minister, the Foreign Minister, the Defense Minister, the Chief of Staff, and the head of military intelligence, the Government ascertained that the armies of Egypt, Syria and Jordan are deployed for immediate multi-front aggression, threatening the very existence of the State."

Evidence that the Israeli invasion was a deliberate act of aggression in collusion with U.S. imperialism for the purpose of overthrowing the Egyptian and Syrian governments as well as territorial conquest does not come so readily to hand. Conspiracies are, after all, not carried on in broad daylight, and many of the facts of this one have yet to be brought to light. But there are definite indications of it. For example, there is the history of Israeli foreign policy which we outlined above, going back to Ben-Gurion's overtures to Dulles. Further, the U.S. assurance of support to Israel clearly implies the existence of a *quid pro quo* understanding. Then there are such items as the fact that the United States and Britain, despite a U.S.-British-French agreement which obligated them to defend Egypt, not only did nothing to halt the aggression but sabotaged UN efforts to do so. In fact, they prevented a cease-fire until Israel had achieved her military objectives.

Little by little the remaining facts will come out, and we have no doubt that they will disclose a no less sordid deal than that of 1956. And they will show further that, as in 1956, a plot to overthrow anti-imperialist Arab governments has failed.

Expansionism Since 1967

The annexationist character of the war is further evidenced by Israeli policy since 1967. In brief outline, its main points are as follows:

1. The Israeli leaders have persistently blocked efforts to find a political resolution of the conflict. Specifically, though claiming to accept it, they have rejected UN Security Council Resolution 242 of November 22, 1967 as the basis for arriving at a settlement.* In

---

* This resolution, after "emphasizing the inadmissability of the acquisition of territory by war and the need to work for a just and lasting peace in which every State in the area can live in security," calls for:

"a) Withdrawal of Israeli armed forces from territories occupied in the recent conflict;

"b) Termination of all claims or states of belligerency and respect for and acknowledgement of the sovereignty, territorial integrity and political independence of every State in the area and their right to live in peace within secure and recognized boundaries free from any acts of force."

On the basis of acceptance by both sides of both these principles, the resolu-

particular, they have refused to commit themselves to withdraw from the occupied territories even in the face of the offer of a peace treaty by Egypt, though they had long declared that such a treaty was their foremost desire.

2. While the Israeli Government has taken no formal stand on withdrawal from the occupied territories other than to declare that it desires no annexations, Golda Meir and other leading government spokesmen have made it clear that extensive areas are to be retained in the name of "secure and defensible" borders. East Jerusalem is "not negotiable." Also to be kept are the Golan Heights, the Gaza Strip and Sharm el-Sheikh with a connecting corridor. The Jordan River is to become a "security border," which means that even if the West Bank is returned to Jordan, Israeli troops are to be stationed along the river while Jordanian troops are to be forbidden access to the West Bank. In short, the Israeli rulers propose to keep possession of a large part of the occupied territory and to retain at least partial control over other areas.

3. While stalling off negotiations endlessly, the Israeli government is carrying out an undeclared policy of *de facto* annexation of the occupied territories through a succession of accomplished facts. East Jerusalem has been annexed outright and is being converted as rapidly as possible into a Jewish city. A string of Israeli settlements has been built along the Jordan River, and numerous others in the Golan Heights, on the northern shore of the Sinai Peninsula, at Sharm el-Sheikh, at Hebron and other localities in the West Bank. The number is steadily growing. In the Gaza Strip a brutal process of displacing the Arab population is under way, supposedly on "security" grounds, but actually with the thinly veiled intention of settling the vacated lands with Jews. The Sinai oil wells have been taken over and are supplying all of Israel's oil requirements. And the economy of the occupied areas is being integrated into that of Israel

---

tion calls for settlement of all outstanding differences. A special UN representative is to be designated to work with both sides to implement its provisions. (Dr. Gunnar Jarring has functioned in that capacity.) The governments of Egypt, Jordan, Syria and Lebanon have stated their acceptance of the resolution *in toto;* the Israeli government has never done so.

along semi-colonial lines, providing Israel with profitable markets
and a source of cheap labor.

4. In violation of the Geneva Convention, the inhabitants of the
occupied territories have been subjected to brutal and repressive
treatment including administrative arrest, collective punishment in
the form of blowing up of houses, interminable curfews, etc., forci-
ble deportations and torture of prisoners. The UN General Assembly has on more than one occasion called for an end to such practices.

Clearly, the aim is to annex most or all of the conquered territories.

These policies have increasingly isolated Israel in the eyes of
world opinion. They have made its future increasingly dependent
on U.S. arms and backing, and in return have subordinated Israel in
growing measure to the interests of U.S. imperialism. They have
imposed huge arms budgets on Israel which are bankrupting the
country financially. And they have led to growing Arab hostility
and the ever-present danger of new outbreaks of war.

Such is the disastrous course on which the Zionist ruling circles
have placed the Israeli people.

3. ISRAEL AND AFRICA

A Pro-Imperialist Policy

Israeli spokesmen have made much of Israel's role as a supposed
benefactor of the developing countries. But the Israeli government's
policy in relation to these countries is likewise designed to serve the
interests of world imperialism. Their penetration by Israel began in
earnest after the ill-fated Sinai campaign of 1956. It represented an
attempt to break out of the isolation resulting from that debacle and
to establish an international base in the regions beyond the immediately surrounding Arab countries.

These aims were viewed as tied directly to those of the imperialist powers and as dependent on their assistance. Harvard professor
Nadav Safran writes: "If there is any 'realistic' motive in Israel's

program of foreign aid, it is probably to be found in the hope that it will draw tangible rewards from the United States by serving . . . the same objects that that country seeks to promote through its aid program." *(The United States and Israel,* p. 267.)

According to Leopold Laufer *(Israel and the Developing Countries,* p. 18), between 1958 and 1966 ties were established with 38 countries in Africa, 23 in Latin America, 11 in Asia and eight in the Mediterranean area. These relations have included Israeli financial and military aid, loans, investments in joint enterprises and training of personnel. The main area of concentration has been Africa. The number of Israeli experts sent to African countries has grown from 25 in 1958 to 406 in 1966 and some 2,000 today. Of some 14,000 foreign students trained in Israel between 1958 and 1971, about half have been Africans.

In monetary terms Israeli aid to African countries is insignificant (less than half of one per cent of the total aid received). But its strategic impact has been far greater. This impact lies primarily in the ability of Israeli ruling circles to present Israel as a moderate, "third force" form of socialism compatible with "free world" interests, and as a small country which is not an imperialist power. And this has made it possible for the Israeli rulers to act as intermediaries for imperialism, a function which they have extensively performed.

This is evident, first of all, in the character of the countries singled out for attention. In the main, these are countries ruled by neo-colonialist regimes which see in Israel a means of helping to perpetuate the dominance of leaders oriented toward one or another imperialist power. Moreover, they include the Portuguese colonies, Rhodesia, West Africa and—not least—South Africa, countries constituting the remaining base of colonial and racial oppression in Africa.

The aid which Israel gives to these countries is primarily military or paramilitary in character. The Israeli government has become highly proficient in training elite military forces along the patterns which prevail in Israel itself today. Even in the field of agriculture, much of the aid has been in the establishment of paramilitary youth organizations and settlements, patterned after the *gadna* and *nahal*

forms in Israel. The former is a battalion of youth aged 14–18
which engages in sports, camping, hiking, crafts and cultural activities, together with physical labor and paramilitary training. The latter
is an agricultural settlement of young men and women of military age, established in dangerous border areas and including military training. Between 1960 and 1966, formations of these types
were set up in Cameroon, the Central African Republic, Chad, Da-
homey, Ivory Coast, Malawi and Togo.

This is in addition to the direct training of military forces. In
Chad, Israel has trained troops for action against the guerrilla
forces of the National Liberation Front of Chad. In the case of the
Congo (Kinshasa)—now called Zaire—Israel has trained para-
troops, both within that country and in Israel. In 1963, 243 para-
troops sent to Israel for training included General Joseph Mobutu,
now President of Zaire. In Ethiopia, Israel has trained troops to
fight the guerrillas on the Eritrean border and in return has been
granted military bases on islands off the Eritrean coast.

In the Ivory Coast, in Kenya, in Sierra Leone, Israel has been involved in providing arms or military training. In Ghana the Israeli
presence goes back to 1956 and has continued up to the present.
Questions have been raised of its possible involvement in the counter-revolutionary overthrow of the Nkrumah government. Israel currently sells some $20 million worth of arms a year, most of it to Af-
rican countries.*

In Uganda, where Israel assumed all military training in 1956
and in addition supplied a number of planes, former President Milton Obote has charged Israel with complicity in the overthrow of
his government by Major General Idi Amin. It was Amin, reports
Winston Berry, editor of the weekly newsletter *United Nations Report,* who sought Israeli aid. Berry writes:

> While the Uganda Government in the United Nations and elsewhere
> followed the Organization of African Unity in its policies toward the

---

* These data are taken mainly from Sanford Silverburg, *Israel Military and
Paramilitary Assistance to Sub-Saharan Africa: A Harbinger for the Military in Developing States,* Master's Thesis, American University, 1968, as
cited in: Africa Research Group, *David and Goliath Collaborate in Africa,*
Cambridge, 1969.

Middle East conflict (policies calling for Israeli withdrawal from the occupied territories—H.L.), Amin insisted that his junior officers be trained in Israel. He insisted that the Israeli instructors and advisers be retained by the army and airforce. *(People's World,* February 13, 1971.)*

Israeli instructors and advisers have been involved in anti-guerrilla fighting in the Portuguese colony of Angola. Servicemen from Portugal and its colonies have gone to Israel for training. Israel has also supplied much of the arms used by the colonialist forces. Thus, a captured punitive detachment in Angola was found to be armed with UZI submachine guns.

In Nigeria the Israeli government identified itself with the oil imperialism-inspired secession in Biafra. Audrey C. Smock, research associate of the Institute of African Studies of Columbia University, writes:

Up to July 1969, Israel had sent £250,000 of official aid for Biafran relief and dispatched several medical teams. Foreign Minister Abba Eban, spaeking in the Israeli Parliament, stated on July 9 that the Israeli Government had "the duty" to send maximum aid to Biafra. A broadcast on Radio Kaduna (Northern Nigeria) later that month accused Israel of sending tanks, artillery and rockets to Biafra in the guise of relief supplies and of training Biafrans in guerrilla warfare techniques. . . . The *Daily Times* (Lagos) denounced Israel's stand as a "clear case of double-dealing" which violated Nigerian friendship and good will. ("Israel and Biafra: A Comparison," *Midstream,* January 1970.)

From the foregoing the pattern is clear. The Israeli ruling circles are to be found on the side of the forces of colonialism and neo-colonialism, of imperialist machinations against the struggles for national liberation. Today U.S. imperialism, in its quest for strategic

---

* Subsequently the situation was sharply reversed. In February 1972 Amin set in motion a process of severing all ties with Israel, charging that Israeli contractors were "milking Uganda dry." In the following month he made the break complete by refusing to renew all existing agreements between the two countries. The entire corps of Israeli diplomats, military advisers and technicians, numbering some 470 together with their dependents, was expelled. Amin has since distinguished himself by applauding Hitler's slaughter of six million Jews. But this only serves further to show the kind of elements with which Israel's rulers are prepared to ally themselves.

raw materials, is injecting itself increasingly into the African scene, allying itself with the racist regimes in South Africa and Rhodesia and with the Portuguese colonialists against the forces of national liberation. In the pursuit of its imperialist aims, it is assisted in no small measure by the policies of the Israeli ruling circles.

Aside from military involvement, Israeli investments in African countries take the form of partnerships with local investors in which the Israeli share is a minority and is limited to five years, after which the local stockholders are required to buy out the Israeli interest. This approach, says Laufer, has "enabled Israeli companies to enter new markets with relatively small capital investment and under the benevolent protection of the governments of developing countries" (p. 148). It has served as a means of getting around competition from other sources.

The Israeli investors are not private firms but quasi-public corporations mainly under the aegis of the Histadrut's economic arm, Hevrat Ovdim. The chief of these is the construction firm Solel Boneh, whose African projects include, according to Laufer: "Public buildings in Sierra Leone and Eastern Nigeria, the international airport in Accra, luxury hotels in Eastern Nigeria, university buildings and 800 miles of roads in Western Nigeria, and military installations in the Ivory Coast" *(ibid.)*. These, it may be noted, are scarcely top priorities in relation to the needs of the poverty-stricken populations of these countries.

The amount of direct investment is small and is intended to serve largely as an opening for the development of trade. But more important, in these enterprises the Israeli ruling class serves as a "middleman" for U.S. and other imperialist forces in their efforts to penetrate and control the economies of the African countries. The Israeli leaders lend themselves to such schemes since they can pose as being "socialist" yet anti-Communist and hence as being "more acceptable" than the imperialist states themselves. It is in this capacity, also, that the Israeli government has sought to develop ties with the Common Market.

The Israeli insistence on a minority interest in joint ventures also opens the door to U.S. and other imperialist investment. The Soviet writer Y. Kashin notes that

Israel's commitment to provide only 40 or 50 per cent of project costs makes it much easier for American and international banks to get a foothold in Africa, for by means of loans these banks can "indirectly secure most of the majority interest, nominally owned by local governments." *(Jeune Afrique,* No. 485, 1970.) There we discover Israel's secret neocolonialist mission in Africa. ("Israeli Designs in Africa," *International Affairs,* February 1972.)

Characteristic of this role are the operations of the Afro-Asian Institute for Labor Studies and Cooperation, located in Tel Aviv and sponsored by the Histadrut. Its purpose is to provide an intensive, short-term training program for as many African trade union leaders as possible. Launched in 1960 with a $60,000 grant from the AFL-CIO, between 1960 and 1962 it received more than $300,000 in grants and scholarships from the AFL-CIO and affiliated unions, and additional sums from British and other labor organizations. It is well known that these activities of the AFL-CIO were financed by the CIA and were regarded as an integral part of its strategy. Yet today the AFL-CIO continues to be a major financial supporter of the Institute. Its contributions are listed regularly in its convention financial reports.

What is taught in such a school, obviously, is the pro-imperialist and anti-Communist line of George Meany and Jay Lovestone which the CIA has so generously underwritten. The Histadrut is also involved in the Israeli pro-imperialist activities in Africa, as we have noted, through the investments of Hevrat Ovdim.

Ties With South Africa

Especially notorious are the relations of the government of Israel with the ultra-racist apartheid regime in South Africa. Political, economic and military links between the two have been maintained since 1948 and in recent years have been increased. And this has taken place in the face of nearly universal condemnation of the racist barbarism of South Africa's white rulers, and despite numerous UN resolutions calling for severance of relations with the South African Republic until it ends the policy of apartheid.*

* For example, the operative paragraph of General Assembly Resolution 2547 B (XXIV) on "Measures for Effectively Combating the Policies of *Apartheid* and Segregation in Southern Africa," adopted in 1962, *"Calls upon* all those Governments which still maintain diplomatic, commercial, military, cultural and other relations with the racist Government of South Africa and with the racist and illegal minority regime in South Rhodesia to terminate such

South Africa was among the first countries to recognize the State of Israel. In 1953 its prime minister Dr. D. F. Malan visited Israel and was cordially received, despite his record of blatant anti-Semitism and wholehearted support of Hitler during World War II. And on Malan's retirement in 1954, his name was inscribed in the Golden Book as a proven true friend of Israel. The South African ruling circles had only unstinting praise for Israel.

This state of affairs lasted until mid-1961 when Israeli policy in relation to other African countries made it expedient to join in the UN condemnation of apartheid. In the ensuing years relations cooled considerably. But with the 1967 war all was forgotten and relationships became closer and more cordial than ever before. The South African government permitted volunteers to go to Israel to work in civilian and paramilitary capacities, and more than $28 million raised by Zionist organizations was released for transmission to Israel.

The South African Foundation, a propaganda organization representing big business interests, took steps to re-establish its Israeli-South Africa Committee as an instrument for seeking closer economic and political ties between the two countries. The Committee, among other things, arranged a meeting between South African Defense Minister P. W. Botha and Shimon Peres, currently a minister in the Meir government, for the purpose of discussing military affairs. In September 1967 General Mordecai Hod, commander of the Israeli Air Force, addressed a selected group of officers at the Air Force College in South Africa. And in December of that year a group of Israeli officials, businessmen and aviation experts made a tour of South Africa.

In May 1969 David Ben-Gurion and Brigadier General Chaim Herzog visited South Africa to launch a United Israel Appeal Campaign. And within Israel an Israel-South Africa League was formed to press for closer ties with South Africa. Its base is chiefly among the Right-wing elements.

In the economic sphere, Israeli exports to South Africa have ris-

relations immediately in accordance with the relevant resolutions of the General Assembly and the Security Council. . . ." It should be noted that Israel voted for this resolution.

en rapidly, from $1.4 million in 1961 to $4 million in 1967 and $15 million in 1970. South African capitalists were prominent in the "millionaires' conferences" held in Israel since 1967 to seek foreign investment (see below). Recently the mining tycoon Henry Oppenheimer paid a visit to Israel. In this connection it should be noted that the diamond-cutting industry, supplied mainly by the South African firm of de Beers, is an important factor in the Israeli economy and a prime earner of foreign currency. In 1968, diamonds made up 34.4 per cent of the value of Israeli exports.

The roots of Israeli-South African relationships go deeper, however, than immediate economic, political or military interests. They lie in the racist, reactionary character which these two states have in common today. It is not accidental that Prime Minister Jan Christian Smuts was a lifelong supporter of Zionism and a close personal friend of Dr. Chaim Weizmann, or that others after him have likewise been strongly pro-Zionist. The attraction which Israel holds for the racist rulers of South Africa is based on their feeling that Zionism has much in common with apartheid.

Thus, former Prime Minister Hendrik F. Verwoerd stated that the Jews "took Israel from the Arabs after the Arabs had lived there for a thousand years. In that I agree with them. Israel, like South Africa, is an apartheid state." *(Rand Daily Mail,* November 21, 1961.) South African government spokesmen have repeatedly hailed Israel as constituting, together with the Republic of South Africa, the only barrier to the taking over of Africa by "world communism."

On their side the Zionist rulers of Israel are also cognizant of such a community of interests. Today U.S. imperialism, basing itself on countries like South Africa, Rhodesia and the Portuguese colonies, seeks to draw certain other African countries which are under neo-colonialist domination more closely into their orbit and so to establish a base for counter-revolution throughout Africa. Toward this end it attempts to promote "dialogue" between such countries and South Africa, as well as "dialogue" between Black Americans and South Africa.

It is precisely in these countries—Lesotho, Swaziland, Botswana and Malawi—in which South African influence is strong, that Israel has stepped up its development programs. Early in 1971 an Israeli mission visited Zaire, Gabon, Ivory Coast, Ghana and Kenya, all of whose governments (with the possible exception of Kenya) are gravitating toward South Africa. Thus do the Israeli Zionist leaders contribute, together with South Africa, in building a base for U.S. imperialism in Africa.

Brian Bunting, a leader in the South African freedom struggles, appropriately summarizes the situation in these words:

> The Israeli-South African alliance is an alliance of the most reactionary forces in the Afro-Asian world, backed by the forces of imperialism, and designed to hold back the tide of progress, preserve the stronghold of profit and privilege and perpetuate the exploitation of the oppressed masses in the interests of the tiny handful of racists and monopolists who are holding the world to ransom today. *Israel and South Africa are today the two main bastions of imperialism and reaction in the Afro-Asian world. The smashing of the alliance between them must be one of the foremost priorities of progressive mankind today.* ("The Israeli-South Africa Axis—A Threat to Africa," *Sechaba*, April 1970.)

Zionists in South Africa

A particularly shameful aspect of this unsavory picture is the role played by the Zionist-dominated Jewish organizations in South Africa.* The Jewish community in that country, numbering some 120,000, is one of the largest and wealthiest in the world. Overwhelmingly Zionist in its leanings, its financial contributions to Israel are second in size only to those from the United States. To be sure, not all South African Jews are Zionists. Many have been prominent in the liberation struggles and have suffered persecution for their activities as Communists or members of the African National Congress. But these are decidedly in the minority.

The dominant Nationalist Party, strongly pro-Hitler and anti-Semitic during World War II, drastically changed its attitude toward the Jewish community in the immediately ensuing years. This was motivated partly by the search for white solidarity in maintain-

---

* For a detailed and well-documented account, see Richard P. Stevens, "Zionism, South Africa and Apartheid: The Paradoxical Triangle," *The Arab World,* February 1970. The author is Professor of Political Science at Lincoln University in Pennsylvania.

ing apartheid, partly by a fear of the withdrawal of Jewish capital, and partly by sympathy with Zionist policies in Palestine. Accordingly, the government waived restrictions on the export of goods and currency in the case of Zionist contributions to Israel, making them an exception to a usually very strictly enforced law. In return it exacted one vital concession: support of apartheid.

In the face of the unspeakable oppression inflicted on Black Africans and the scarcely less brutal oppression of Coloreds and Indians, the Jewish Board of Deputies and other spokesmen of the Jewish community have maintained total silence. Not even the horrible massacre at Sharpeville in 1960 evoked so much as one word of protest. The official position of the Board of Deputies in such matters was stated to be one of "non-intervention." Dan Jacobson, a prominent South African Jewish writer, defended this position, saying that other religions condemn apartheid because they have Black adherents, but there are no Black Jews. Hence the Jewish community "raises its voice when its own immediate interests are threatened . . . and for the rest keeps mum." (Dan Jacobson and Ronald Segal, "Apartheid and South African Jewry: An Exchange," *Commentary,* November 1957.)

But it has been more than a matter of "keeping mum," which is bad enough in itself. Not only was Malan honored by Israel; when Verwoerd became prime minister in 1958 a delegation from the Board of Deputies conveyed formal congratulations. Later, at the time of Verwoerd's death, the Chief Rabbi said of him that "a moral conscience underlay his policies: he was the first man to give *apartheid* a moral ground." *(Rand Daily Mail,* September 12, 1966.) In short, the official spokesmen for the Jewish community have become outright apologists for apartheid.

In this shameful stand they have been upheld by their colleagues abroad. World Zionist organizations, and particularly those associated with the Jewish advisory body to the UN, have carefully refrained from comment on the question of apartheid and from any criticism of the South African Jewish organizations for their support to it. Typical of the justification offered for this is the following statement by Rabbi Morris Pearlzweig, speaking for the World Jewish Congress:

The non-government Jewish organizations refrain from responding on the problems of South Africa because they do not want to make the situation of South African Jewry difficult . . . and they know that this policy is very much appreciated by the Jewish community there. Moreover, the constitution of the World Jewish Congress does not permit any involvement in Jewish affairs of Jewish communities that have the freedom of self-expression, unless by explicit demand or permission of the Jewish community concerned. (Quoted by Baruch Shepi in "Israel, Zionism and South Africa," *Zo Haderekh,* May 19, 1971.)

As we shall see, no such delicate scruples are shown in the case of the Soviet Jews.

Such is the disgraceful record of Zionism in relation to this most hideous form of racism. And such is the role of the Israel-South Africa axis in fostering the aims of imperialism in Africa.

4. AGENTS OF IMPERIALISM

Zionist Intelligence Services

The Zionists have also played the role of secret agents for imperialism on a world scale. Of the extent of this assistance during World War I, Jacob de Haas, a former secretary to Herzl and a U.S. Zionist leader during the war years, writes:

. . . The great strength of the American Zionist organization was in the multifariousness of its contacts, and in the accurate knowledge of those in control of the human resources on which they could depend. Did the British need to obtain a contact in Odessa, or were they in need of a trustworthy agent in Harbin?

Did President Wilson require at short notice a thousand-word summary detailing those who were in the Kerensky upheaval in Russia? The New York office rendered all these services, asking nothing, but receiving much, the respect and good will of men whose signatures counted in great affairs. (*Menorah Journal,* February 1928. Cited by Daniel Mason in the *Daily World,* May 23, 1970.)

An especially shocking case of such espionage during World War II is that of the Polish Revisionist Zionists. These had migrated to Palestine and there, under the leadership of Menachem Beigin, had formed the National Military Organization, later known as Irgun

Zvai Leumi. Of their activities Frank Gervasi, an avowed Zionist sympathizer, writes:

> When Polish troops were evacuated from Russia to the Middle East by way of Palestine in 1941–42, connections among the Palestinian Revisionist Party, the N.M.O. and their Polish confreres of the old days were re-established. They had new reasons now to resume business. The rightwing Poles fear and hate Russia and Communism. Their Dwoika, or secret service, enlisted the help of the N.M.O. and the Revisionists in identifying pro-Russian elements in the Polish army. They also asked the Revisionists to help them disseminate anti-Russian and anti-Communist propaganda through their well-established channels in Britain and the United States. *(To Whom Palestine?*, pp. 32–33.)

Today the Israeli secret service performs a similar function. And it is reputed to be a highly effective organization. According to a UP dispatch by Joseph W. Griggs (December 31, 1969), Israel's "agents are scattered throughout the world." Ray Vicker, writing in the *Wall Street Journal* (February 12, 1970), speaks of "Little Israel's ability to create an espionage network with world-wide scope, operational capability, efficiency and individual talent rivalling that of far larger powers. . . ."

This network has been placed at the disposal of U.S. imperialism, and in exchange the Israeli government has received the benefit of the fruits of U.S. Intelligence. Thus, David Ness, who was U.S. Chargé d'Affaires in Cairo at the time of the 1967 war, writes in *The Times* (London) on February 5, 1971:

> In the exchange of intelligence, American cooperation with Israel is unprecedented. . . . During the months before the June, 1967, hostilities, the military intelligence requirements required by Washington from American embassies, the Central Intelligence Agency and military intelligence staffs in the Middle East were very largely based on Israel needs, not on American interests. The effectiveness of the Israel air strikes on June 5, 1967 was assured, at least in part, by information on Egyptian airfields and aircraft disposition provided through American sources. With political and economic information, it has long been State Department practice to provide the Israeli Embassy in Washington with copies of all of our reports from Middle East embassies considered to be of interest.

Israeli training of specialized and elite military personnel in African and other countries entails the training of security forces in the techniques of protecting the neo-colonialist regimes in these countries against the danger of popular overthrow. These activities undoubtedly place the Israeli government in a position to cooperate with Washington on intelligence matters in these areas also, although this cooperation quite naturally remains shrouded in secrecy.

Imperialist Alliances—A Disastrous Course

To sum up, Israel's Zionist leaders, seeking to establish the security of the State of Israel through a policy of aggressive expansionism at the expense of the Arab peoples, have placed Israel in league with the forces of imperialism, and today above all of U.S. imperialism. They have made Israel's destiny increasingly dependent on the fortunes of U.S. imperialism in its own aggressive designs in the Middle East.

But such a policy can lead only to disaster for the Israeli people. It brings Israel into ever sharper conflict with the world forces of anti-imperialism and progress which are constantly gaining in strength. And it ties Israel's future to the sinking ship of imperialism, which continues to lose ground to these forces in the Middle East as it does elsewhere.

Moreover, history has shown the imperialist powers to be highly unstable allies. The British imperialists, having issued the Balfour Declaration, then proceeded to abandon the Zionists and to use the Mandate to play Jews and Arabs against each other in typical "divide and rule" fashion. As we have seen, Britain opposed the UN partition resolution and later incited its puppet rulers in the Arab states against Israel. In the 1956 war, Israel was allied with Britain and France but opposed by the United States. Today Israel is tied very closely to U.S. imperialism, while its relations with French ruling circles have greatly cooled. Thus, the position of these imperialist states has shifted between support and opposition as their interests have dictated.

The primary concern of these powers in the Middle East is not Israel's well-being but the defense of the interests of the powerful oil monopolies. Israel is useful to them only insofar as its role serves this end. Should support of Israel come into direct conflict with these imperialist interests, it is undoubtedly Israel which would be considered expendable. Hence the present Israeli policy, which places Israel more and more at the mercy of U.S. imperialism, holds forth prospects not of security but of endless warfare in which Israel, despite its present military superiority, must in the end be destroyed.

Such is the reactionary, suicidal character of the Zionist-dictated policy of the Israeli government.

III

ORGANIZED ZIONISM
IN THE UNITED STATES

1. ZIONIST ORGANIZATIONS AND ACTIVITIES

The Zionist Movement

In the pursuit of their Zionist policies the Israeli leaders rely in no small measure on the support of the organized Zionist movement throughout the capitalist world, and especially in the United States.

On a world scale the official spokesman for Zionism is the World Zionist Organization. In Israel this body has quasi-governmental status based on the Israeli Status Law of 1952, which says:

. . . The State of Israel recognizes the World Zionist Organization as the authorized agency which will continue to operate in the State of Israel for the development and settlement of the country, the absorption of immigrants from the Diaspora and the coordination of the activities in Israel of Jewish institutions and organizations active in these fields.

The Israeli government also looks upon the World Zionist Organization as an instrument for winning support for Israeli foreign policy abroad.

In the United States, bourgeois influences among the Jewish people have grown enormously during the past few decades. Jewish nationalism has greatly increased and the influence of Zionism has become widespread, especially since the 1967 war.

In the early part of this century, however, political Zionism met with little acceptance among U.S. Jews. It was opposed by Orthodox religious leaders as contrary to the precepts of Judaism, which taught that the return to the Promised Land was to occur only with the coming of the Messiah. It was opposed by Reform Jewish leaders and others as bringing the loyalty of Jews to the United States into question, and by class-conscious Jewish workers as contrary to their class interests and destructive of the fight for socialism.

"As late as 1914," writes Robert Silverberg, "there were only 12,000 dues-paying Zionists among the 3,000,000 Jews of the United States. The annual budget of the whole American movement was $12,150." (*If I Forget Thee O Jerusalem*, p. 60.)

Zionism's first spurt of growth came immediately after World War I, stimulated by the Balfour Declaration and by a wave of anti-Semitism in the United States, exemplified by the notorious anti-Semitism of Henry Ford's newspaper, the *Dearborn Independent*. Later, with the rise of Hitlerism and especially with its mass slaughter of Jews, the Zionist movement grew very rapidly. Indeed, it was only with this genocidal persecution of Jews that Zionism became a mass movement; it was their common persecution which became the chief bond among Jews in different lands. After World War II the establishment of the State of Israel gave further impetus to Zionist influence and the 1967 war brought it to its highest point.

Today, avowedly Zionist organizations in the United States claim a combined membership of some 750,000. The largest is the Women's Zionist Organization of America (Hadassah) with well over 300,000 members. Second largest is the Zionist Organization of America (ZOA) with 100,000. Prominent among the numerous other Zionist organizations are the United Labor Organization of America (Poale Zion), the Religious Zionists of America (Mizrachi) and the Americans for Progressive Israel-Hashomer Hatzair.

Of those organizations which refer to themselves as "non-Zionist," the largest is B'nai B'rith, a men's fraternal and religious organization with more than 500,000 members. Other influential organizations include the American Jewish Congress and the American Jewish Committee. The leaders of these and other such organizations are today in the main Zionist in outlook and the organizations themselves are no less active in support of the Zionist policies of Israel's rulers than are the explicitly Zionist organizations.

The American Jewish Congress is affiliated with the World Jewish Congress, which is an important adjunct of the World Zionist

Organization. Its current president, Nahum Goldmann, defines its
function as being "to symbolize and make a reality of the common
resolution of the Jewish people to unite in defense of its rights; and
to secure the cooperation of the various branches of this dispersed
people in matters of common interest." (*The Autobiography of Nahum Goldmann,* p. 125.) But the "common interest" around which
the Jewish people are to be united is Zionism, and the World Jewish
Congress plays the same "non-Zionist" role on a world scale as its
affiliate does in this country.

Other pillars of Zionist support are the synagogues and temples,
whose total membership is very considerable. And not least, Zionism boasts the support of Jewish Right-wing social democracy as
embodied, for example, in the Jewish Labor Committee and the
Daily Forward, both of them rabidly anti-Communist and anti-Soviet.

To be sure, the movement is by no means homogeneous. The
American Jewish Committee was anti-Zionist in its origins and
bears traces of this today. Similarly, in organizations like B'nai
B'rith and in the religious institutions, as we shall see, exceptions
and conflicting trends exist. But overwhelmingly, they are characterized by their support of Zionism.

Zionism also relies heavily on the backing of non-Jewish allies.
Prominent among these is the Meany clique in the leadership of the
AFL-CIO. This group has consistently supported Israeli policy, rec-
ognizing it as being in keeping with U.S. imperialist interests in the
Middle East. The Histadrut, as we have already noted, maintains
close working relations with the Meany-Lovestone axis. And the
AFL-CIO Executive Council is among the most vociferous support-
ers of all-out military aid to Israel.

In 1970 an American Zionist Federation was formed, seeking to
capitalize on the increased support for Zionism since the 1967 war.
It includes among its affiliates 13 adult and 10 youth Zionist organizations and it also provides for individual memberships, thus permitting individuals to join the organized Zionist movement without
having to join an organization identified with a particular political
party or grouping in Israel.

Fund-Raising and Politics

Since 1948, "aid to Israel" has become the chief focus of activity among U.S. Jews. Scores of millions of dollars are raised every year, sums large enough to be a vital factor in the Israeli economy. The United Jewish Appeal, an umbrella fund-raising organization reports that from 1948 to the end of 1970 a grand total of nearly $1.5 billion, some two-thirds of all funds raised in that period, had been allotted to the United Israel Appeal. Of the rest, which went almost entirely to the Joint Distribution Committee, an organization dispensing assistance on a world scale, a substantial part was also spent in Israel. In addition, considerable sums are raised by a number of individual organizations. Hadassah alone sends more than $10 million a year to Israel.

During the 1967 war an emergency fund of $175 million was raised almost overnight, and in 1968 an added $85 million was collected. At the same time, from 1951 to the end of 1970 nearly $1.4 billion worth of long-term Israel bonds were sold in the United States out of a world total of $1.64 billion. On this huge inflow Israel has been heavily dependent for its economic survival.

Accompanying these mammoth fund-raising drives is an uninterrupted flood of political activity, aimed at securing support for the policies of the Israeli government. In the major centers of Jewish population, and especially in New York City, the big Jewish organizations wield not a little influence in the political arena. Witness, for example, the refusal of New York State's Governor Nelson D. Rockefeller and New York City's Mayor John V. Lindsay to receive President Pompidou of France on his visit in 1970—a refusal prompted by the public demonstrations organized by Jewish groups. Witness also the fact that in late 1971 no fewer than 88 U.S. senators signed a petition calling on the Nixon Administration to deliver Phantom jets to the government of Israel (a bill to this effect was soon afterward passed by an overwhelming majority in the Senate).

Because the Jewish population is concentrated in the biggest cities and in key states from an electoral standpoint, the Jewish organizations are able to make themselves strongly felt in national elections. It would be a rash presidential candidate indeed who would dare openly to oppose Zionism or Israeli government policies. We may note, in this connection, the almost frantic efforts of Senator George McGovern, in his campaign for the U.S. Presidency in 1972, to outdo President Nixon in identifying himself with Israel's ruling circles. There is also a well-organized lobby in support of the Israeli government, which a *New York Times* article (April 6, 1970) describes as "one of the most potent in the Washington sub-government." The article says further: "The foundation stones of the pro-Israel lobby are an embassy that is generally considered the best run in Washington and scores of Jewish organizations which have large amounts of manpower, money and zeal."

As a result of these pressures (and of the absence of comparable pressures from the Arab side), and because it accords with U.S. imperialist policy to build Israel's Zionist regime up as a champion of "Western civilization" and the "free world," the communications media have joined with U.S. ruling circles in presenting to the American people a completely one-sided, chauvinist and essentially false picture of "little Israel" as an oasis of light and progress in a desert of Arab backwardness—an oasis, moreover, which is constantly threatened with physical extinction by the surrounding Arab hordes. And there are few to challenge this mythology.

Ties with the Israeli Government

We have already noted the quasi-governmental status of the World Zionist Organization in Israel. With this body, and with particular political parties and other groupings in Israel, the various Zionist organizations in this and other countries are affiliated. And thereby they have come to serve as agencies of Israeli government influence abroad.

The ties of these organizations, as well as those of "non-Zionist" organizations, with the Israeli government are maintained through the Jewish Agency for Israel. This body was originally established under the British Mandate as a governing body of the Jewish settlement in Palestine, under the aegis of the World Zionist Organization. After the establishment of the State of Israel its official status was preserved in the Status Law of 1952 and in a Covenant signed by the Israeli government and the leaders of the WZO in 1954.

Today it continues to exist as a sort of shadow government made up of representatives of the various Zionist political parties in Israel plus a number of representatives from abroad. It bears specific responsibility for promoting immigration and for the integration of immigrants and operates independently of any democratic controls within Israel. It does, however, cooperate with the Ministry of Absorption in the Israeli government. Recently it was reconstituted to provide for much greater representation from abroad.

As noted above, some two-thirds of the funds raised yearly by the United Jewish Appeal are turned over to the United Israel Appeal, which allocates them on the basis of a budget prepared by the Jewish Agency in Israel. They are distributed through the office of the Jewish Agency in New York. The three organizations—UJA, UIA and the Jewish Agency—work closely together and, as Lawrence Mosher notes in an article in the *National Observer* (May 18, 1970), their leaderships overlap. Thus, at the time of the article, of two officers of the Jewish Agency registered with the State Department as agents of the Israeli government one was also a vice-chairman of UIA and the other was a member of its board of directors and a former president of Hadassah. In addition, the executive vice-chairman of UIA was also a secretary of UJA.

At the other end, much of the money distributed by the Jewish Agency goes to political parties in Israel and to the institutions controlled by them. Of this, Uri Avnery writes:

> Several million dollars are parcelled out directly among the Zionist parties, ostensibly as compensation for relinquishing their rights to organize their own fund-raising in the United States. But this represents only a small fraction of the real division; by financing youth organizations, educational activities, propaganda agencies, and other institutions belonging to the Zionist parties, the Jewish Agency goes a long way toward sustaining the huge apparatus that every Zionist party maintains in Israel and abroad. (*Israel Without Zionists,* p. 175.)

Much larger sums are spent by the Jewish Agency for its own operations in connection with immigration.

A considerable share of the money raised here finds its way into the treasury of the Israeli government, to be used in pursuit of its own aims. And the bulk of it provides the government with desperately needed foreign exchange to pay for arms acquired from the United States.

At the same time, substantial sums of money are funneled back to this country via the Jewish Agency, to be used for propaganda in support of the Israeli government. These operations usually go unpublicized, even though federal law requires that propaganda activities for or on behalf of foreign governments or other foreign principals be publicly disclosed. As an illustration, Mosher, in the article cited above, points to the Zionist magazine *Midstream,* published in New York by the Herzl Foundation. *Midstream,* he states, "is subsidized by the Jewish Agency in the amount of $96,000 a year. Emanuel Neumann, chairman of the magazine's editorial board, is one of the two persons who are registered foreign agents for the Jewish Agency's American office." But no reader of *Midstream* would ever know this from the magazine itself.

In 1963 a Senate Foreign Relations Committee investigation of the American Zionist Council (a coordinating body for a number of Zionist organizations) found that it was acting as a "conduit" for the Jewish Agency, having received over an eight-year period more than $5 million for the purpose of creating favorable public opinion toward the Israeli government's foreign policy. The investigation put a stop to this particular operation but the propaganda continues, financed through other, less obvious channels.

The American-Israeli Public Affairs Committee, Zionism's Washington lobby headed by I. L. Kenen, was registered as a foreign agency up to 1951. Since then it has not been registered although both its structure and activities remain unchanged.

All contributions to the UJA, be it noted, are tax-deductible even when the money goes for such political purposes. It was against these practices that the well-known writer on foreign affairs, the late James P. Warburg, rebelled a number of years ago. In a speech made in November 1959, he objected to using UJA funds to support Israeli state policy, saying:

. . . it is a great mistake for the United Jewish Appeal to refuse—as it has refused for years—to segregate funds contributed for relief or for cultural purposes from funds destined to flow directly or indirectly into the Israeli treasury. I have several times protested against this high-handed procedure; and since I, for one, have been unwilling to support the Israeli state so long as it pursues some of its present policies, I have had no choice but to discontinue my contribution. . . .

Why should all contributions to the United Jewish Appeal be tax-deductible when so large a proportion of them flow directly or indirectly into the hands of a foreign government which openly engages in propaganda attempting to influence the policy of the government of the United States? It seems to me that, unless the United Jewish Appeal changes its policy of mingling all contributions, it will sooner or later lose its tax-exempt status, as indeed, in my judgment, it should. ("Israel and the American-Jewish Community," *Jewish Currents,* January 1960.)

But the UJA retains its tax-exempt status. Nor is the U.S. government likely, as long as the Israeli government's policies serve the interests of U.S. imperialism, to make an issue of how the UJA uses the funds it raises.

What is most shocking, however, is the fact that the major Jewish organizations, Zionist and non-Zionist alike, play the role of political arms of the Israeli government. To some extent this role is openly acknowledged. Thus, Mosher quotes Rabbi Jay Kaufman, executive vice-president of B'nai B'rith, as writing to a fellow staff member: "BB [B'nai B'rith] is now playing a greater role in the fate and future of Diaspora Jewry, assuming the tasks which the State of Israel cannot legitimately undertake because it is a sovereign state and cannot intrude in the affairs of other nations."

In June 1970 Sol E. Joftes, dismissed after 22 years as a B'nai B'rith official, sued the organization for breach of contract and its two top officers for libel. The suit was based on two letters by Rabbi Kaufman charging him with incompetence and failure properly to perform his duties. The real reason for his dismissal, Joftes asserted, was that he had fought efforts to convert B'nai B'rith from a charitable and welfare organization into an unregistered agent of the Israeli government. He cited in evidence the employment of a Mrs. Avis Shulman, whose job was to brief Jews about to visit the Soviet Union and to pass information obtained on these visits to the Israeli government.

As of the time at which this is written, Joftes has already won a $35,000 judgment for back salary and severance pay and $12,000 for "interference" with his contract by Rabbi Kaufman. The libel suit was denied but is still under appeal. But whatever the courts may ultimately decide as to the merits of his particular allegations, there are clear indications that B'nai B'rith maintains a relationship with the State of Israel which goes much beyond the charitable or the religious.

Indeed, organized Zionism as a whole behaves as an arm of the State of Israel, openly or covertly, supporting not only its right to exist but its specific policies through financial, propaganda and other channels.

2. ARE THEY REALLY ZIONISTS?

The Conflict in World Zionism

Central among the tenets of Zionism is that Israel is the homeland of all Jews and hence it is incumbent on Jews everywhere—at the very least on Jews who consider themselves Zionists—to migrate to Israel. According to Ben-Gurion, Zionism can have only one meaning: "to Zion." In his address to the 25th World Zionist Congress in December 1960, he delcared that since the founding of Israel "every religious Jew has daily violated the precepts of Judaism . . . by remaining in the Diaspora." Jews, he maintained, can truly live as Jews only in Israel, and "there cannot be a full and complete Jewish culture in the Diaspora, even in those free countries which grant Jews every right."

This concept is fundamental in the thinking of Israel's Zionist ruling circles. As Avnery puts it:

The fundamental tenets of Zionism can be defined as follows: (a) all the Jews in the world are one nation; (b) Israel is a Jewish state, created by the Jews and for the Jews all over the world; (c) the Jewish dispersal is a temporary situation, and sooner or later all Jews will have to come to Israel, driven, if nothing else, by inevitable anti-Semitic persecution; (d) the Ingathering of these Exiles is the *raison d'etre* of Israel, the primary purpose to which all other aims have to be subservient. This line is taught in Israeli schools, propounded in political speeches, written in the daily press. It is the essence of the existing regime *(op. cit.,* pp. 157–58).

Aliya—migration to Israel—is the incessant demand of the Israeli leaders. But this demand has met with a pitifully small response from U.S. Jews. As of 1967 the total number of Jews from this country living in Israel was a mere 15,000. Since the 1967 war the rate of migration has considerably increased, but even with this the present total is no more than about 35,000.* Moreover, writes Georges Friedmann: "According to an official statement made by the Israeli immigration services (January 10, 1967) 50 per cent of the immigrants coming from the United States have, since the creation of the State, returned to their own country of origin. Among them, recently, was a high proportion of skilled non-manual personnel who were unable to find openings in the Israeli economy." (*The End of the Jewish People?*, pp. 231–32.)

Indeed, says Friedmann, up to 1967 the emigration from Israel to the United States was much greater than in the opposite direction. Douglas L. Greener, writing in *Israel Magazine* (May 1971), states: "While North American Jews are going to Israel in increasing numbers, there are today around 100,000 Israelis living here in America. Many are students who will complete their studies and return home. But 25,000 Israelis have become United States citizens since 1956."

The failure of U.S. Jews (and Jews from other Western countries as well) to migrate to Israel in significant numbers has given rise to a resentment among Israeli Zionist leaders which not even the millions in contributions serve fully to erase. Despite their devotion and generous support to Israel, these Jews, they maintain, are not really Zionists since they do not accept Zionism's mandate to live in Israel.

On the other hand, U.S. Zionists insist that their Zionism is no less genuine than that of the Israelis, and the controversy has on more than one occasion become very acrimonious. At a meeting of world Zionist leaders in 1968, for example, Izhak Korn, secretary of the Labor World Zionists, proposed that membership in the

---

* These figures are based on unofficial estimates. The Israeli government publishes no official figures. Moreover, they include those who come to Israel to retire as well as those who come to work and participate actively in the country's economic life.

World Zionist Organization be confined to those Jews who commit themselves and their families to migrate to Israel within five years. This provoked vehement opposition from the U.S. representatives, with the president of Hadassah denying that "a Zionist is only one who is committed to living in Israel." The proposal was defeated.

The conflict came sharply to a head at the 28th World Zionist Congress in January 1972, where a resolution was introduced by a group of young Israeli Zionists stating that Zionist leaders "must set an example for every Zionist by implementing their ideals and coming to Israel themselves. If they do not go on Aliya within two terms of office they cannot continue to hold office." After a stormy debate the resolution was passed by a vote of 104–95, whereupon nearly the entire Hadassah delegation walked out. Since a rift with Hadassah, with its huge financial contributions, was unthinkable the matter was patched up, at least for the time being, by having the resolution declared unconstitutional.

At the same time, the idea that U.S. Zionists are not truly such, in one variant or another, is also expressed by not a few in Jewish circles here. Thus, the well-known writer on Jewish affairs Judd L. Teller states:

> We speak of a defunct Zionist movement in America. . . . Actually there has never been a Zionist movement in America. . . . What we had was a movement of pro-Zionists, and that is why we faced a crisis in 1948. Everyone became pro-Zionist then. If it had been an ideological movement, it would have faced no crisis. However, Zionist ideology had not been accepted; some sections of the Zionist program were accepted, but not Zionist ideology. ("The Failure and Prospects of U.S. Zionism," *Israel Horizons*, April 1970.)

The Jews who came to this country from Europe, says Teller, have chosen their homeland and it is the United States, not Israel. And since the chief function of Zionist organizations has become aid to Israel, others contend, there is no point to their continued existence since non-Zionist organizations perform this function just as well.

Indeed, with the establishment of the State of Israel in 1948, membership in Zionist organizations fell off considerably. That of the ZOA dropped from 200,000 to 100,000. The reason generally given for this decline is that Jews who wished to support Israel found that they could readily do so without assuming the political commitments involved in belonging to Zionist organizations.

Consequently, the idea that U.S. Zionists are not really Zionist but are only "pro-Zionist" has gained considerable currency. It is, however, an erroneous view.

To begin with, it should be noted that despite the decrease after 1948, membership in explicitly Zionist organizations has remained impressively large. And since 1967 support for Zionism has grown.

Further, not all Zionists accept the thesis that Israel must literally and physically become the homeland of all Jews. Ahad Ha'am, the father of spiritual Zionism, looked upon Palestine as the *spiritual* homeland of world Jewry, as a cultural and religious center for Jewish communities everywhere, providing a basis for the preservation of their Jewish identity. Nahum Goldmann, president of the World Jewish Congress and for a number of years also president of the World Zionist Organization, has expressed a similar view:

. . . We shall find some new way of continuing the intimate, fateful relationship between the state and the people, the center and the periphery, and thus acquire the spiritual strength to guarantee the survival of the Jewish communities in the Diaspora. The situation of the Jews will never be normalized through a state alone, but only by creating a center in Palestine while at the same time retaining the great Diaspora, linked with the state in an enduring and mutually enriching relationship *(op. cit.,* p. 79).

This concept has its adherents both in Israel and the United States, some of whom refer to it as a "new Zionism." Sanford Goldner describes it as follows:

Until recently the philosophy of Zionism involved the notion of "the ingathering of the exiles"; Jewish life in any land but Palestine was doomed to destruction. However, the divergence of this philosophy from reality became increasingly evident as American Jews, who had become the bulwark of financial and moral support for Israel, showed no disposition to settle in Israel. Now theory has caught up with practice, in American Zionist circles at least. The "new Zionism" is based on the "permanence of the Diaspora," with Israel as the cultural center of the various settlements of Jews throughout the world. *(Perspectives in American Jewish Life,* pp. 80–81.)

There has thus developed the concept of a permanent interde-
pendence between the State of Israel and the Jewish communities in
other countries, particularly in the United States. More important,
within this framework U.S. Zionists *do* accept the basic precepts of
Zionism such as the concepts of a world Jewish nation, of the permanence of anti-Semitism and of a Jewish state which is exclusively
Jewish and is the homeland of Jews everywhere. The Jewish state is
central, the *sine qua non* for the preservation of Jewish identity in
the Diaspora. And they fully support the reactionary, aggressive
policies of the Israeli rulers stemming from these concepts.

Indicative of an outlook which is widespread in Jewish circles
here and in Western Europe are the views expressed by George
Steiner, British literary critic and author. Steiner was the opening
speaker in the Sixth Annual American-Israel Dialogue, sponsored
by the American Jewish Congress and held in Israel in July 1968.

He professes internationalism and argues that Jews must progressively "free themselves from the myths of nationalism and proclaim
that, whereas trees do indeed have roots, human beings have legs
with which to move among each other." *(Congress Bi-Weekly,*
February 24, 1969, p. 15.) Jews, he says, have learned to live and
flourish within Gentile communities and have become, of necessity,
an international people.

However, Jews have never been more than "guests" in these
communities; they are condemned to be aliens in the countries in
which they live. "Post-exilic Jews," says Steiner, "have always been
suspect to their hosts." He adds that "each of us in the Diaspora
knows that we are guests on sufferance" and that "the relationship
of the Jew to his nationhood is a vulnerable one." And further, "no
Gentile nation-state will ever fully accept its Jews or keep its bar-
gains of safeguard with them in times of political or economic crisis" *(ibid.,* p. 14). The rise of the State of Israel only strengthens
the suspicion of the Jew, the feeling that he is a person of divided
loyalties.

But Israel is, by the same token, vital to Steiner and his family as
a potential haven from the ever-present threat of persecution.
"Where but in Israel," he asks, "will my children find refuge when
the next pogroms start in, say, Rabat or Argentina or, perhaps,
Mississippi?" *(ibid.,* p. 17). Note that he says "when," not "if."

These views dovetail remarkably with those attributed by Avnery, above, to the Israeli Zionists. Yet Steiner was attacked as an opponent of Zionism, particularly by some of the Israeli participants in the dialogue, on the grounds that he did not find migration to Israel an immediate necessity.

The Zionists in this country accept the Zionist concept of an exclusively Jewish state and the anti-Arab chauvinism which flows from it. It is precisely this kind of state which the American Jewish Congress, in its declaration of purposes, seeks to help "develop in peace, freedom and security."

Moreover, the U.S. Zionist Establishment has become notorious for its slavish adherence to every detail of Israeli foreign policy. The idea prevails that the Israeli government must be supported no matter what it does, since Israel is *their* state—the *Jewish* state. So much is this so that even some leading figures within Zionist circles have been moved to protest. Rabbi Maurice N. Eisendrath, writing in *Dimensions* (Fall, 1970), deplored "the spectacle of a supinely submissive and self-suppressed American Jewry," adding: "Not a peep of protest against a single scintilla of official Israeli foreign policy is permitted by the Jewish Establishment of America."

Similar protests from other sources could be cited. They give testimony to the fact that the dominant forces in the complex of Jewish organizations—financially, politically, ideologically—are devoted adherents of Zionism. To argue about whether they are "Zionist" or "pro-Zionist" is mere quibbling. Of the reactionary influences of this dedication to Zionism on the Jewish community as a whole we shall speak later.

The Myth of "Good" and "Bad" Zionism

There are some within the Jewish Left who claim to find positive elements in Zionism and who seek to differentiate between "good" and "bad" Zionism, "good" and "bad" Zionists.

This approach is developed by Paul Novick, editor of the Yiddish daily, *Morning Freiheit*. In a speech delivered in January 1957 he stated:

There is no question that from the very beginning of the Zionist movement, many spokesmen of political Zionism cooperated with imperialism or let themselves be used by it. But it is just as certain that the masses of followers of the Zionist movement in old Russia and Pilsudski Poland saw in Zionism a way out of their woeful lot and thought it held a solution for the Jewish people. . . .

To repeat, it is necessary to distinguish between one Zionist tendency and another, between leaders and followers and also between one leader and another. It should be kept in mind that together with a number of religious leaders, many Zionist leaders in America have played a positive role in the fight for civil rights, against segregation, against the McCarran-Walter Law, and even against the Smith and McCarran Acts. *(Jewish Life in the United States,* pp. 17, 18.)

Novick continues to express the same ideas today. Thus he says: "We oppose political Zionism that cooperates and supports the State Department. But there are other Zionists, such as Rabbi [Arthur J.] Lelyveld, who oppose the State Department, who oppose the war in Vietnam." *(Morning Freiheit,* April 5, 1970.) And more recently:

The Zionist movement consists of various trends. It is necessary to try to cooperate with Zionists in the struggle against war, against racism, for the United Nations resolution (No. 242) on the Middle East. He who does not understand this, who approaches the problem dogmatically and throws everybody into one pot, harms the struggle against imperialism, chauvinism and reaction among the Jewish masses. *(Morning Freiheit,* May 14, 1972.)

But all this is sheer sophistry, serving to cover up an opportunist conciliation of Zionism. Are there differences among Zionists? Of course there are. Are there Jews who support Zionism in the sincere belief that it serves the best interests of the Jewish people? Of course there are. Are there Zionists who oppose U.S. aggression in Indochina? Of course there are. Is it possible to work with Zionists on common issues? Of course it is. But all this has nothing to do with the nature of Zionism as such.

Novick confuses subjective desire with objective reality. The intentions and desires of individual Zionists, however laudable they may be, in no way alter the reactionary, racist character of Zionism itself.

There are not two kinds of Zionism, one pro-imperialist and the other anti-imperialist. To be sure, the opposition of Rabbi Lelyveld to the war of U.S. imperialism against the people of Indochina is to be greeted. So too is his participation some years ago in the Mississippi freedom campaign, in the course of which he was severely beaten by racist thugs. But all this does not render his Zionism any less objectionable. His active support to the racist Zionist conception of a Jewish state, to the aggressive, pro-imperialist policies of Israel's rulers and to Washington's imperialist role in the Middle East, and the leading part which he has played as president of the American Jewish Congress in the fraudulent campaign against alleged "Soviet anti-Semitism," must be condemned no less than in the case of anyone else.

There are people in the United States who are out-and-out racists but who are at the same time strongly opposed to the Indochina war. But is their racism any less harmful than that of those who support the war? Is it any less an obstacle to the unification and strengthening of the peace movement? Clearly the fight for peace is inseparable from the fight against racism—*within the peace movement itself.* By the same token, the fight against the aggressive policies of U.S. imperialism in Southeast Asia is inseparable from the fight against its aggressive policies everywhere else, including the Middle East. One cannot condone the support of a Lelyveld to U.S. imperialism in the Middle East on the grounds that he opposes it in Indochina without weakening the entire struggle for peace. Furthermore, while it is of course necessary to distinguish between leaders and followers, it is obviously not possible to win the followers of Zionism away from the poisonous influence of its leaders, to win them to the cause of peace and progress, without striving to expose Zionism for what it is, and without clearly recognizing that it is Zionism *as such* which is reactionary, not just the position of some of its leaders.

To fail in this, to suppress the fight against Zionism in the name of unity in the struggle to end the war in Indochina, is to weaken this struggle as well. For Zionist support of U.S. imperialism in the Middle East impairs the fight against its aggressions elsewhere.

This is shown in the widespread retreat of Jewish organizations and leaders from the fight against the Indochina war. Some years ago, opposition to the war in Jewish circles was far more outspoken —indeed, so much so that in September 1966 President Johnson, angered by it, made a none too subtle effort at blackmail. He intimated to a group of Jewish leaders that aid to Israel might be cut off if such opposition continued. His effort met with a sharp rebuff. However, since the 1967 war the situation has changed considerably.

Top Israeli spokesmen like Golda Meir and Moshe Dayan openly support the U.S. aggression in Indochina, and their stand is parroted by certain leading Zionists in this country.* Jacques Torczyner, former president of the Zionist Organization of America, has called upon American Jews to support the war, arguing that they cannot otherwise expect U.S. support to Israel, also that the stakes in Vietnam and the Middle East are the same.

An editorial in the ZOA organ, *The American Zionist* (November 1969) spells this out. Today, the editorial asserts, it is the Soviet Union and China which are seeking the ends formerly pursued by the Axis powers. "It can no longer be denied," it states, "that Communism has taken the place of Nazism as the sworn enemy of the Jewish people." It adds: "Only the United States stands between them and the realization of their designs." Hence "neither the cause of Jewry, nor the cause of American democracy, nor for that matter the cause of peace, is served by the prominent appearance in the peace movement of Jewish spokesmen."

Others do not take such an extreme position, but nevertheless exert pressure against participation of Jewish organizations and leaders in peace activities. Rabbi Balfour R. Brickner, himself an active opponent of the Indochina war, has noted with dismay that

many American Jewish "peaceniks" who only a few months ago were conspicuously vocal in opposition to their government's conduct of the war in Vietnam now seem to have lost their tongues, silenced by a fear

* The position of Golda Meir is revealed with particular clarity in a message of congratulations to Nixon on his statement of U.S. policy in Vietnam on November 3, 1969. The statement, transmitted through the U.S. ambassador to Israel, reads: "The Prime Minister wishes to congratulate the President on his meaningful speech, and express her hope that he will speedily succeed in bringing about peace in Vietnam. The President's speech contains much that encourages and strengthens freedom-loving small nations the world over, which are striving to maintain their independent existence looking to that great democracy, the United States of America." (*The New York Times,* November 17, 1969.)

—whether imagined or real—that such criticisms might jeopardize American political or military support for Israel. ("Vietnam and the Jewish Community," *Christian Century,* April 29, 1970.)

"The silence of Jewish spokesmen," he said, "is deafening."

Rabbi Brickner expressed profound disturbance at the atrocities committed by U.S. military forces, the Nazi-like racist attitudes toward the Vietnamese people, the morally corrupting callousness which such actions and attitudes were producing among the American people. "How would we as a nation fare," he asked, "were we to be judged by the Nuremberg principles we imposed on the Germans in 1945? What has happened to our national conscience when we apparently can endorse the 'acting under orders' rationale we utterly condemned in 1945?" Yet, he noted, 1,500 Jewish leaders could meet in January 1970 on the "erosion" of U.S. policy in relation to Israel, without once mentioning the question of Israel and Vietnam.

This is not to say that the Jewish people are absent from the fight for peace. On the contrary, like other sections of the American people they are overwhelmingly for immediate withdrawal of all U.S. military forces from Indochina. They have participated along with others in the struggles to attain this goal, and a number of leading Jewish figures have been especially active and outspoken. Among major Jewish organizations the American Jewish Congress and the Central Conference of American Rabbis have come out in opposition to the war.

Nevertheless, the role of Zionism in its fight for support to U.S. imperialism in the Middle East has been to weaken Jewish participation in the fight for peace. And to the extent that they uphold this Zionist line, the effectiveness of even those Jewish leaders who are outspoken for peace is diminished, as it is also by such things as their role in the shameful campaign of anti-Soviet slander, in which they are also leaders.

Failure to combat Zionism, therefore, and the preaching of ideological coexistence with Zionists in the name of "united front," detracts from the struggle for peace and progress. It is exactly in this direction that the opportunist thesis of "good" Zionism and "good" Zionists leads.

3. THE ROLE OF MONOPOLY CAPITAL

Jewish Capital and Israel

Spearheading the Zionist movement in the United States today is a major section of the big Jewish capitalists. This group has provided the lion's share of the contributions which have helped the Israeli government to finance its enormous military expenditures. It is the main purchaser of Israel bonds. It has made substantial investments in Israel and has been a leading participant in the three "millionaires' conferences" held in Israel since 1967 for the purpose of securing increased foreign investment. And it has exercised preponderant ideological influence within the movement. Indeed, it is its class interests which are served by Zionism with its preaching of class peace.

It would be wrong, however, to regard Zionism as a movement initiated by the Jewish bourgeoisie. On the contrary, the main sections of Jewish big business were originally strongly anti-Zionist and assimilationist in their views. Part of them, including such Jewish families of finance capital as the Lehmans, Morgenthaus, Rosenwalds and Warburgs, became involved in Palestine from philanthropic and business standpoints. Only later, after the establishment of the State of Israel, did any considerable number of them become pro-Zionist. At the same time another grouping, associated with the American Council for Judaism, has remained completely anti-Zionist and assimilationist.

From the very outset the Zionists looked to the Jewish capitalists to finance their colonialization schemes, beginning with the settlements in Palestine supported by Baron Edmond de Rothschild in the 1880s and 1890s. In 1902 the Jewish National Fund and the Jewish Colonial Trust were established under the aegis of the World Zionist Organization as the Zionist movement's chief financial instruments. The purpose of the former was to raise funds for the purchase of land; the latter was set up as a bank with its headquarters in London. Among its stated purposes were "to promote, develop, work and carry on industries, undertakings and colonization schemes" and "to seek for and obtain openings for the employment

of capital in Palestine, Syria, and any other part of the world."
(Survey of Activities and Financial Report, 1899–1922.) Both ap-
pealed to Jewish capitalists as the chief source of funds. Aaron
Cohen notes:

> As for the Jewish Colonial Trust, in 1908 it had a paid-up capital of
> £225,000, of which £36,000 was invested in the Anglo-Palestine Bank
> in Jaffa and another £15,000 in the Anglo-Levantine Banking Company.
> The Trust's board of directors opposed risking this money in direct in-
> vestments in Palestine, and gave all too few money grants-in-aid to settle-
> ment projects." *(Israel and the Arab World, p. 41.)*

The Trust's career was not a distinguished one. After the Mandate, investments were made in a number of ventures in Palestine,
among them the General Mortgage Bank, Bank Hapoalim and Palestine Electric Corporation. In 1933 it was reorganized, handing
over its banking and investment operations to the Anglo-Palestine
Bank (now Bank Leumi Le-Israel) and has existed since only as a
holding company for that bank.

Subsequently other vehicles for Jewish capital investment in Palestine and later in Israel were established in the form of investment
corporations, particularly in the United States. Prominent among
these has been the Palestine Economic Corporation, which now
designates itself as PEC Israel Economic Corporation. It was
founded in 1926 under the sponsorship of the top Jewish financial
groups, Kuhn-Loeb and Lehman Brothers. Felix Warburg, then
senior partner in Kuhn-Loeb, became its largest stockholder. PEC
was an offshoot of the American Jewish Committee, founded in
1906 by a group of Jewish bankers and industrialists, chiefly of
German origin, and representing some of the most reactionary and
most assimilationist sections of Jewish big capital. They were, however, evidently not averse to profitable investments in Palestine.
The American Jewish Committee also became dominant in the
United Jewish Appeal, thus combining philanthropy and profitable
investment.*

Lehman Brothers and Kuhn-Loeb have retained an interest in
PEC Israel Economic Corporation. As late as 1961 Herbert H.

---

* For a more detailed account of these interrelationships in their initial
stages, see A. B. Magil, *Israel in Crisis*, pp. 101–07.

Lehman was honorary chairman and Edward M. Warburg was a vice president of the board of directors. In 1969 the honorary chairman was Robert Szold, a leading founder of PEC, whose family has been associated with Lehman Brothers.

The present chairman of the board is Joseph Meyerhoff of Baltimore, a big real estate operator and a director of the Beneficial National Life Insurance Company and of several Israeli banks. Among the board members is Eli M. Black, chairman of the board and president of the two-billion-dollar conglomerate AMK Corporation, which owns United Fruit Company. Another, Ludwig Jesselson, is president of the Philipp Brothers Division of Engelhard Minerals and Chemicals Corporation, prominent in South African gold mining. A third, M. L. Mendell, is a director of Interstate Department Stores, Inc., retired vice president of Bankers Trust Company and treasurer of Rogosin Industries, Ltd., leading manufacturer of synthetic fibers in Israel.

At the close of 1969 PEC held $24.3 million in investments and loans in some 45 Israeli enterprises, including some of the largest. It recorded a net profit of $1,104,000 for the year, an increase of nearly 27 per cent over the year before.

In July 1969 the IDB Bankholding Corporation, Ltd. was formed in Israel, a conglomerate-type company listing as its two subsidiaries the Israel Discount Bank and the PEC Israel Economic Corporation, and as affiliates four other Israeli banks. With a combined capitalization of more than $45 million and combined resources of some $950 million, the IDB Bankholding Corporation is the largest private enterprise in Israel.

There is considerable interlocking between PEC and the Israeli Discount Bank. Raphael Recanati, a managing director of the latter, is also a vice chairman of the PEC's board of directors. Another member of this financially prominent Israeli family, Daniel Recanati, is chairman and a managing director of the Israel Discount Bank and a member of PEC's national advisory board. Two other PEC directors are also directors of the bank. Several are directors or officers of IDB Bankholding Corporation.

"The Holding Corporation," the 1969 PEC Financial Report states, "will be dedicated and equipped to pursue the original objective of PEC—the development of the Israeli economy on a sound business basis." Which, of course, means a profitable one. At the same time, says the Report, "PEC will continue as an American company."

There are a number of other corporations serving as vehicles for investment by U.S. Jewish capitalists in Israel. Among them is the Israel Investors Corporation with $22 million invested in Israeli enterprises, including a 50 per cent interest in the *Jerusalem Post* and $4.4 million of holdings in IDB. Other U.S.-based investment companies include AMPAL American Israel Corporation* and Israel Research and Development Corporation. To facilitate these and other operations there are several Israeli and Israeli-American banks with offices in New York, among them Bank Leumi Le-Israel, Israel American Industrial Development Bank, Ltd., Israel Discount Bank, Ltd., First Israel Bank and Trust Company of New York and Republic National Bank of New York (controlled by the Israeli-owned Safra bank of Switzerland).

All this, it is clear, adds up to a very sizeable interest of U.S. Jewish capitalists in Israel's economy.

The Stake of U.S. Imperialism

Financial support to Israel, however, is not limited to Jewish capital and other Jewish contributors. Since its birth, Israel has received well over $1 billion in grants and credits from the U.S. government, in contrast to less than $60 million received by a country like Syria. Nor are investments in Israel restricted to Jewish capital. Of the more than $1 billion of investments to date by U.S. capitalists, the major part is in the hands of non-Jewish capital. More than 200 U.S. firms have invested in Israel, including 30 of the top 500 U.S. industrial corporations. Among these U.S. investors are such familiar names as Ford, Chrysler, Monsanto Chemicals, Motorola, International Business Systems, Holiday Inns, American Can, Control Data, General Telephone and Electronics, Xerox Data Systems, National Cash Register and others.

U.S. monopoly capital is a dominant factor in the Israeli econo-

---

* AMPAL provides credits to and has direct investments in Histadrut enterprises, notably COOR, Solel Boneh and Bank Hapoalim.

my today. More than half of all foreign capital invested in Israel is American. A great part of Israel's financial, industrial and commercial institutions are in American hands. Of Israel's enormous foreign debt, 80 per cent is owed to the U.S. government and to U.S. organizations and institutions. Of its large annual trade deficit, some 40 per cent is incurred in unequal trade with the United States. This includes the huge purchases of arms of which the United States is now overwhelmingly Israel's chief supplier.

In 1971 alone the Israeli government received a $500 million loan from the United States for the purchase of Phantom jets and other arms. And President Nixon has made it clear that his administration is prepared to supply Israel with all the arms required to "maintain the balance of power" in the Middle East—that is, Israel's military superiority. But the $500 million and all other debts incurred for military goods must be repaid—and in U.S. dollars, not in Israeli pounds. Israel, it is clear, pays both an economic and political price for its government's reliance on U.S. support.

It is U.S. imperialism *as such* which has bolstered (and dominated) the Israeli economy and has supplied Israel with arms. It has followed such a policy because it accords with the interests of the dominant sections of U.S. finance capital in the Middle East, with their desire to use Israel as a weapon against the Arab liberation movement and its threat to U.S. oil investments. In this picture the top Jewish financiers play an important role, together with their counterparts in other capitalist countries. But it is at the same time a subordinate role. Powerful as they are, the big Jewish capitalists are a minor factor in the totality of U.S. finance capital. Moreover, they are relegated to a peripheral status, thanks in part to the anti-Semitism which prevails in Wall Street as it does elsewhere in U.S. society. Of this, Victor Perlo writes: "The anti-Semitism of Wall Street . . . has had the . . . objective of keeping the Jewish bankers 'in their place' as intermediaries with the world of trade and light industry, a role from which the top oligarchy also derives substantial profits." *(The Empire of High Finance,* p. 186.)

Thus, the Lehman-Goldman, Sachs finance capital group has its main center of interest in retail commercial enterprises and the food and other light industries. Of total assets of $5.8 billion controlled by this group, $2.8 billion are accounted for by the following firms:

Federal Department Stores, General Foods, National Dairy, Gimbel Brothers, May Department Stores, Sears, Roebuck and Company, McKesson and Robbins, McCrory Corporation, Allied Stores and General Baking. At the same time its orbit includes also such firms as American Metal Climax, Continental Can, General Dynamics and Owens-Illinois Glass, as well as Lazard Frères which acts as bankers for International Telephone and Telegraph and other corporate giants. Similarly Kuhn, Loeb has banking ties with the Rockefeller interests. (S. Menshikov, *Millionaires and Managers,* pp. 266, 298–99). Here we see both their subordinate status and their ties with the top finance capital groups.

This in no way lessens the leading role of the big Jewish capitalists in the Zionist picture. Rather it indicates the centrality of Zionist dependence on U.S. imperialism and the fact that the role of Jewish capital is exercised in relation to this.

Dependence on Foreign Capital

Instead of seeking economic independence, Israel's ruling class has from the beginning tied the country's economy to foreign capital, chiefly U.S. and British. Since the 1967 war economic dependence on U.S. imperialism has grown considerably. In 1968–1970, U.S. government subsidies and loans, together with private investments and contributions, totalled almost half of the total import of capital.

Today, with the burden of military expenditures threatening Israel with economic bankruptcy, and with an increasingly desperate demand for foreign currencies, a way out is being sought through greatly increased foreign investment. Toward this end, three "millionaires' conferences" were held in Israel between 1967 and 1969, attended by representatives of foreign capital. These gave birth in 1968 to the Israel Corporation, an investment company whose purpose was to attract foreign capital. Its goal was $100 million, but by the end of 1970 it had succeeded in scraping together only $21 million.

The fact is that the inflow of private capital has fallen off markedly in recent years, while the outflow of profits has risen. In 1965, net foreign investment was $113 million while repatriated profits totalled $94 million. In 1970, net investment had fallen to $55 million while repatriated profits had jumped to $165 million. Moreover, capital investment has been increasingly devoted not to establishing new enterprises but to buying into already existing government-owned firms such as the ZIM Steamship Line. Israel Oil Refineries, Timna Copper Mines and Palestine Potash.

To secure these investments the Israeli government has willingly disposed of its holdings to a point where it has little left to sell. Thus, the Israel Corporation now owns 50 per cent of ZIM and 26 per cent of Israel Oil Refineries. Israel's first jet engine plant, Beit Shemesh Engines, Ltd., is owned 49 per cent by the Israeli government and 51 per cent by the French Turbomeca Company. And General Telephone and Electronics has a 35 per cent interest in Tadiran Electronics, with the remaining 65 per cent held by the Ministry of Defense and Histadrut.

To encourage foreign investment the government has also offered fantastic concessions, among them grants and long-term credits up to twice the amount invested, generous tax concessions, exemption from payment of duties on required imports, payment of export premiums, payment of half of research and development outlays, full rights of repatriation of principal and interest, and others. Thanks to these lavish grants and loans the actual value of foreign holdings is often as much as three times the amount invested.

The largest new venture is the Eilat-Ashkelon oil pipeline, built at a cost of $120 million. Its present capacity is 20 million metric tons a year (a metric ton is 1.1 U.S. tons), and is expected to reach 60–70 million tons a year by 1975. By way of comparison the Suez Canal in 1966, its last full year of operation, carried 176 million tons. Such a pipeline is clearly not required by the Israeli economy; its purpose is rather to provide the foreign oil monopolies with an alternative route to the Suez Canal (in this connection there is also talk of building an Eilat-Ashdod canal). And though the pipeline was built mainly with government funds it is operated as a concession by a subsidiary of Canadian A.P.C. Holdings, Ltd.

Thus does the Israeli ruling class barter away the country's economy to foreign monopolies and subject Israel to increasing imperialist domination. For U.S. monopoly capital, including Jewish capital, Israel exists primarily as another arena of exploitation, of the extraction of superprofits at the expense of the Israeli working people, to be milked for all it is worth. As a source of comparatively low-priced skilled and technical labor, it provides a profitable base of production of certain types of goods for export to Asian and African countries. Through these channels much of the money raised by the United Jewish Appeal in this country finds its way into the coffers of U.S. monopoly capital, Jewish and non-Jewish. This is the reality cloaked by high-sounding, hypocritical declarations of undying dedication to Israel's welfare.

IV

A BULWARK OF REACTION

1. THE STRUGGLE AGAINST ANTI-SEMITISM

How Zionism Downgrades the Struggle

In the opening chapter we presented the Zionist conception of the Jewish question. It is, of course, quite at odds with the Marxist conception.

The Communist Party of Israel defines the Jewish question in these words:

> When we talk of the Jewish question, we mean the question of the discrimination, persecution and even annihilation (especially under Nazi rule) of Jews for being Jews. The problem of the solution of the Jewish question is, therefore, the problem of liberation of the Jewish masses from the virus of anti-Semitism, which appears in various forms in the society of class exploitation. The problem is, therefore, how to uproot the virus of anti-Semitism completely, how to ensure the Jewish popular masses freedom and equality of rights. ("The Jewish Question and Zionism in Our Days," *Information Bulletin, Communist Party of Israel,* Nos. 3–4, 1969, p. 187.)

National and racial oppression are instruments of capitalist exploitation, and national chauvinism and racism are forms of capitalist ideology designed to perpetuate that exploitation. They are means of dividing workers, of pitting workers of differing race and nationality against one another, not only to maintain the superexploitation of the working people of oppressed nationalities but to intensify the exploitation of the workers of the oppressing nation itself.

Like other forms of chauvinism and racism, anti-Semitism is an instrument of reaction, of the capitalist exploiters for sowing dissension among the people and dividing the working class. The struggle against anti-Semitism is part of the struggle for working-class unity, for democracy, against the class forces of reaction in our society. It is part of the struggle against all forms of racial and national oppression. Historically the Jewish people have long been victims of persecution and the horrors of the Nazi holocaust are all too real. But they are by no means the only victims. Countless millions of Africans suffered death at the hands of slave traders and colonialists. The genocidal extermination of Indian peoples in the Western Hemisphere by colonialists and the advancing forces of capitalism is a matter of record. The Hitlerites are responsible for the death of twenty million Soviet citizens, of more than three million Poles and of many others in addition to the Jews. And today U.S. imperialism is engaged in the brutal mass slaughter of Vietnamese. Such mass murder and genocide are basic features of imperialism. To defend the rights and well-being of the Jewish people, therefore, it is necessary to defend the rights and well-being of all peoples.

Such is the Marxist view. It is based on recognition of the class roots of anti-Semitism and of the class struggle and working-class unity as the primary vehicles for its eradication. Zionism, on the contrary, views the Jewish question entirely apart from its class roots. Therefore it looks upon anti-Semitism as eternal and as a unique form of oppression.

In the Soviet Union and other socialist countries the Jewish question has been resolved with the elimination of the monopoly capitalist roots of chauvinism and racism. Of this we shall have more to say later.

In the United States, on the other hand, anti-Semitism is a problem of considerable proportions, both in its "respectable" forms and in the highly virulent forms propagated by the fascist ultra-Right. Professor Charles Y. Glock, who headed an extensive study of the subject by the University of California Research Center from 1960–1965, summarized its conclusions in these words:

One third of Americans are not anti-Semitic at all. Another third have anti-Semitic beliefs but are not vocal or active about it. The last third are outspoken anti-Semites. Included in the last group is the one in ten Americans who advocate doing something to take "power" away from the Jews. *(Time,* December 17, 1965.) *

A survey by the American Jewish Committee in 1969 showed that in history and social studies textbooks used in junior and senior high schools, expressions of prejudice against Jews are common. Other surveys disclose widespread exclusion of Jews from top executive and administrative positions in colleges and universities, public utilities, industrial corporations, banks and other business institutions. There is also extensive discrimination in other employment, in college enrollments, in housing and in other aspects of Jewish life.

With the sharp swing toward reaction on the part of the Nixon Administration, and with the growing aggressiveness of the ultra-Right, fascist elements, has come a rise in open, virulent expressions of anti-Semitism. The circulation of vicious anti-Semitic filth has increased. Desecration of synagogues and similar actions have become more and more common. Financed by the dollars of "respectable" billionaire corporations, and finding fertile ground in the "respectable" anti-Semitism so widely prevalent in this country, the ultra-Right purveyors of racism and anti-Semitism hold forth the ever-present threat of a flareup of violent anti-Semitism.

Clearly, anti-Semitism in the United States is not a minor matter. Zionism, however, habitually downgrades the struggle against this real anti-Semitism. One finds no mass campaigns against its manifestations such as are organized for the "deliverance" of Soviet Jews. On the contrary, such actions are frowned upon, on the specious argument that they would only stir up the anti-Semites and make matters worse.

Actually, Zionism gives encouragement to anti-Semitism. First, it accepts the premise of the anti-Semites that Jews can never become full citizens of the lands in which they live. Illustrative is the following statement by Dr. Farrel Broslawsky, chairman of the Los Angeles chapter of Americans for Progressive Israel-Hashomer Hatzair:

---

* For a detailed account of these studies see Charles Y. Glock and Rodney Stark, *Christian Beliefs and Anti-Semitism,* Harper and Row, New York, 1966.

. . . in America, as in every Diaspora situation, Jewishness is a socially defined set of attributes forced upon individuals according to the dictates of society. It is not possible for the individual to assert himself subjectively as a Jew, nor is it possible for the individual to escape being objectively defined as a Jew. The social system removes the element of choice and forces a functional definition upon the individual. Since one cannot help being defined as a Jew, his only choice is to struggle against the social definition as a form of existential self-assertion. In the United States, most Jews have refused the option of struggle and have acquiesced in the system's objective definition for the sake of material benefits and the illusion of assimilation. . . .

But no matter how much the Jew attempts to become thoroughly assimilated into American society, the tension between the subjective and objective definitions prevents his acceptance by the rest of society. He may seek to deny his heritage, but the social system persists in identifying him as the Jew. As the social system objectively needs the Jew, so the Jew must continue to exist. He has no choice. ("Those of Us in Babylon," *Israel Horizons,* November 1971.)

This is simply an elaborate way of saying that the Jew must continue to be singled out as an alien element in American society, no matter what is his desire to be accepted.

It is, in effect, a sort of anti-Semitism in reverse, attributing to non-Jews as such the very same incompatibility that anti-Semites attribute to Jews as such. That is, Zionism and anti-Semitism both are rooted in racist concepts.

At the same time, Zionism relies on anti-Semitism as the cement which will hold Jews together as a distinct entity and bring them eventually to Israel. Any lessening of anti-Semitism is looked upon as opening the doors to assimilation and loss of Jewish identity. Indeed, assimilation is viewed as the chief threat to the Jewish people today. Speaking at the 26th Congress of the World Zionist Organization in 1964, Nahum Goldmann, then its president, stated:

. . . We are now living in a period when a very large part of our people, especially the younger generation, is threatened by an anonymous process of erosion, of disintegration . . . by lack of challenges which would arouse Jewish consciousness and make it evident why they should remain Jewish. . . .

This process, if not halted and if not reversed, threatens Jewish survival more than persecution, inquisition, pogroms, and mass murder of Jews had done in the past.

And, of course, nowhere does this terrible fate threaten Jews more than in the Soviet Union. Such a view, to put it mildly, is hardly conducive to fighting anti-Semitism. For Zionists the rise in anti-Semitic propaganda in the United States is not half as serious as the rise in intermarriage.

Suppression of the struggle against anti-Semitism has characterized Zionism throughout its existence. It became especially glaring with the rise of Hitlerism in the thirties. The mounting horrors of Hitlerite anti-Semitism evoked growing outrage and resistance among the Jewish people generally. The Zionist organizations, too, were impelled to oppose and combat it. But this came into conflict with the basic attitude of Zionism toward anti-Semitism, and it was the latter which predominated. Hence it was that leading Jewish organizations and spokesmen opposed any forthright expressions or demonstrative actions against the mounting horror of Hitlerite anti-Semitism in Germany on the grounds that this would only arouse the Hitlerite elements in the United States. Instead, millions of dollars were sent to Hitler for the relief of German Jews.

Nahum Goldmann writes:

> We complain today that the non-Jewish world did not take an effective moral and political stand against the Nazi regime but embarked instead upon years of appeasement and had to pay the price with the Second World War. Historically these charges are completely justified, but no less justified is the self-accusation of our people, which irresolutely and myopically watched the coming of the greatest catastrophe in its history and prepared no adequate defense. We cannot offer the excuse that we were attacked unexpectedly. Everything Hitler and his regime did to us had been announced with cynical candor beforehand. Our naiveté and complacent optimism led us to ignore these threats. In this mortifying chapter of Jewish history there is no excuse for our generation as a whole or for most of its leaders. We must stand as a generation not only condemned to witness the destruction of a third of our number but guilty of having accepted it without any resistance worthy of the name. *(The Autobiography of Nahum Goldmann,* pp. 147–48.)

This attitude continued even when Hitler's plans for the extermination of Jews became known. Weizmann encountered it on a visit to the United States in 1940, now projected in the name of maintaining "neutrality" and avoiding "war propaganda." He writes:

. . . Now for the first time rumors began to reach us of plans so hideous as to be quite incredible—plans for the literal mass extermination

of the Jews. . . . It was like a nightmare which was all the more oppressive because one had to maintain silence: to speak of such things in
public was "propaganda"! (*Trial and Error*, p. 420.)

But it went much further than this. Speaking at a symposium in
1966, Knesset Member Chaim Landau stated: "It is a fact that in
1942 the Jewish Agency knew about the extermination . . . and
the truth is that they not only kept silent about it but silenced those
who knew." (*Ma'ariv*, April 24, 1966.)

He could have said much more. As the trial involving Dr. Rudolf
Kastner held in Jerusalem in 1952 revealed, there was actual collaboration with the Nazis. Kastner had to admit that he and others,
knowing that Hungarian Jews were being sent to the gas chambers,
agreed not only to keep this silent but also to help "pacify" the victims in exchange for the promise of the Nazi hangman Adolf Eichmann that a small number of selected Jews would be permitted to
migrate to Palestine.

Eichmann himself describes Kastner's role in these words:

. . . This Dr. Kastner was a young man about my age, an ice-cold law-
yer and a fanatical Zionist. He agreed to help keep the Jews from re-
sisting deportation—and even keep order in the deportation camps—if
I would close my eyes and let a few hundred or a few thousand young
Jews to emigrate illegally to Palestine. It was a good bargain. For keeping order in the camps, the price of 15,000 to 20,000 Jews—in the end
there may have been more—was not too high for me. . . . And because Kastner rendered us a great service by helping keep the deportation camps peaceful, I would let his groups escape. After all, I was not
concerned with small groups of a thousand or so Jews. ("Eichmann's
Own Story: Part II," *Life*, December 5, 1960.)

At the same time, Kastner was involved in efforts to save a small
number of Jews, mainly Zionist leaders and wealthy pro-Zionists, in
exchange for foreign currencies, trucks and military goods. But he
was by no means alone in these Zionist operations. Thus, Jon and
David Kimche relate the case of two Palestinian Jews, Pino and
Bar-Gilad, who got the agreement of the Gestapo in Berlin and Vi-
enna to set up pioneer training camps for young Jews to migrate illegally to Palestine. The Kimches state: "These two Jewish emissar-
ies had not come to Nazi Germany to save German Jews. Their
eyes were fixed entirely on Palestine and the British Mandatory."
(*The Secret Roads*, p. 27.) They report also that Eichmann established an office, run by him, for illegal migration to Palestine.

Such is the sorry record of Zionism in relation to the Hitlerite slaughter of Jews.

A "New Anti-Semitism"

Since the 1967 war the Zionists have discovered a "new anti-Semitism"—an "anti-Semitism of the Left." Lothar Kahn, writing in the *Congress Bi-Weekly,* organ of the American Jewish Congress, spells it out in these words:

> For the first time in modern history, the Jew is imperiled from both the Left and the Right. . . . For the Left, the anti-Jewish course is hidden under the political label of anti-Zionism. It has been used by much of the Marxist camp, the so-called neutrals, and by Black Power groups and their sympathizers. It has served as a respectable political cover by Arabs inflaming their people to a new frenzy; by Communist states frustrated by their inability to assimilate Jews fully and exterminate every vestige of religious-cultural identity; by African nations eager to prove their solidarity with the anti-imperialist, socialist Soviet-Nasser bloc; by American Black extremists merging their pro-Moslem bias with the charge of Jewish capitalism and exploitation. Young Jewish radicals, in the forefront of the various movements, have through their silence backed the anti-Zionist campaign as part of the anti-Establishment, anti-imperialist package they have bought, possibly with some misgivings. ("The American Jew in the Seventies," March 6, 1970.)

The New York Times (November 29, 1969) cites Nahum Goldmann as speaking in a similar vein. It reports: "In place of the 'classic anti-Semitism of the old-line reactionary forces,' extremist elements of the New Left have engaged in such forms of anti-Semitism as attacking Zionism and equating Israel with 'colonial imperialism,' Dr. Goldmann said."

The device is obvious: to be anti-Zionist is to be anti-Semitic. On these spurious grounds the Soviet government, since it opposes Zionism, is declared to be anti-Semitic. And the anti-Zionism and pro-Arab sympathies that are widespread among Black Americans are declared to be evidences of a menacing "Black anti-Semitism."

Thus, notes Michael Selzer, statements by Black organizations condemning Israeli aggression are denounced as anti-Semitic. He states:

> The race relations coordinator of the American Jewish Committee told this writer bluntly: "We will cease to cooperate with any Negro

organization which comes out with an anti-Israel stand; we regard such a stand as anti-Semitic." *(Israel as a Factor in Jewish-Gentile Relations,* p. 3.)

On the basis of such a criterion, "anti-Semitism" is found to be widespread indeed among Black people. The preface to the book *Negro and Jew: An Encounter in America,* containing a collection of articles from the magazine *Midstream,* opens with the following:

It is now accepted as an incontrovertible fact that, 1) there exists a pronounced anti-Jewish sentiment among the Negro masses in this country, despite the active participation of many idealistic young Jews in the Negro struggle for Negro rights, and the moral support given to the Civil Rights Movement by organized Jewish groups, and 2) that Jews are reacting to this with an emotional backlash.

This fiction of "Black anti-Semitism" has been magnified into a monstrous threat to U.S. Jews. Now, indeed, it is none other than the Black Americans who are alleged to be the persecutors of the Jews. Thus, Milton Himmelfarb writes in the publication of the American Jewish Committee, *Commentary* (March 1969):

Is the president of the teachers' union a Jew? Then call him a Zionist and warn him that he will not be allowed to perpetrate in Harlem the genocide that the Israelis are supposed to be perpetrating in the Middle East. . . .
If that is not bad enough, the quota system is being introduced. Or reintroduced—only this time not, as in the universities and professional schools of the 1920s, to keep those pushy Jews (greasy grinds) from dispossessing the gentlemen, but to do justice to Negroes.

Here the quota systems imposed on Jews by the dominant Anglo-Saxon ruling-class elements are flatly equated with the efforts of the oppressed Black people to secure some degree of equality in education through compensatory measures. The fact that they have suffered discrimination infinitely worse than has ever been imposed on Jews in the United States is totally ignored. The mere demand for a higher percentage of Black administrators, teachers and college students becomes the imposition of a quota system on Jews.

Such distorted views have emerged with particular sharpness in relation to the educational system in New York City, where the teaching and administrative personnel is chiefly Jewish. They were expressed in the shameful, racist strike of the United Federation of

Teachers in 1969, led by President Albert Shanker and his cohorts —a strike directed against the Black and Puerto Rican peoples seeking to obtain some semblance of decent education in the ghettos through community control of the schools. The Shanker attack was marked by the wholesale distribution of propaganda charging "Black anti-Semitism."

These views came to the fore again in 1971 with the decision of the Lindsay Administration to conduct an ethnic census of New York City's employees. The census was welcomed by Black and Puerto Rican spokesmen as a means of determining the extent to which these groups are excluded from city employment, especially in the higher-paying jobs. But it was energetically opposed by a number of leading Jewish organizations. Indicative of the character of this opposition is the following, appearing in a column in *Israel Horizons* (March-April 1972) whose author signs himself "Y'rachmiel." Responding to a column in the leading Black newspaper *Amsterdam News* by its executive editor Bryant Rollins, in which Jewish opposition to the census is challenged, he states that

if Mr. Rollins thinks the Jews are fighting the questionnaire because they are afraid for their jobs and their livelihood, he is exactly right. I don't find it written in any law, religious or secular, that it must be the Jews, and the Jews alone, who are to make way for the upward mobility of the Blacks. If Mr. Rollins is looking for whipping boys, I would ask him to look elsewhere. We Jews have played that role much too long—longer by millenia than have the Blacks.

Here, instead of seeking to unite Jews and Blacks in common struggle against the ruling-class instigators of discrimination against both, Y'rachmiel pits one against the other and looks upon the employment status of Jewish teachers and administrators as something to be defended against the encroachment of Blacks and Puerto Ricans. Such a contest serves only the interests of the real racists and anti-Semites and undermines the struggle against them. In these circles, representing the interests of the giant monopolies, lie the sources of the growing retrenchments in an already grossly inadequate educational system while military expenditures continue to soar. But the Y'rachmiels, in the fashion typical of narrow nationalism and Zionism, see *only* the interests of the Jews and view all other peoples as their enemies.

Such views are carried to their ultimate extreme by the so-called "Jewish Defense League." "Anti-Semitic black racists," it asserts, "are battling for control of the cities. . . ." And this grave menace must be fought, arms in hand. Of this fascist gang and its actions we shall have more to say later.

Not surprisingly, the major Jewish organizations and their leaders have with few exceptions steered clear of the struggles in recent years against the brutal persecution of the Black Panthers and other Black militants. And they totally boycotted the fight for the freedom of Angela Davis. Judd Teller, writing in *Congress Bi-Weekly* (November 20, 1970), declares:

Even if it were true that the Black Panthers are the victims of a judicial conspiracy—and this is yet to be proven, even as their guilt is yet to be proven—there are a number of questions that a Jew should consider before striking an instant liberal posture. Is there not good reason to fear that the monies for the Black Panthers' defense will be deflected to their political purposes, even as were the monies raised by the Communists in the 1930s for the defense of both real and fictitious victims of that time?

Apart from his slanderous allegations, Mr. Teller is among those who find fictitious stories of political repression in the Soviet Union real, and real cases of repression in the United States fictitious or questionable. He goes on to say:

The abstention of Jews from contributing to the Black Panthers' defense or from conducting their defense will not jeopardize the outcome of their case. Jews are a very small percentage of the population. . . . Moreover, the Black Panthers are anti-Israel and anti-Jewish. Beneath all the euphemisms the two positions remain identical.

That they are victims of racist persecution and frameups (which the actions of juries in freeing them have by now made clear to everyone), and therefore deserve to be defended by all who are seriously anti-racist and who cherish democratic liberties, is apparently of no matter. They are anti-Zionist (which Teller equates with being anti-Israel) and therefore anti-Semitic, and this is what really counts. And anyhow, the weight of the Jewish community is inconsequential—a specious argument which, interestingly, is never raised when it comes to "freeing" Soviet Jews.

All the more was this attitude displayed in the Angela Davis case. She is a Communist, it was asserted, hence an anti-Zionist and hence an anti-Semite. And so it is that virtually no major Jewish organization, no Jewish religious congregation, no important Jewish leader spoke out in her defense. And not a few took a negative view of her acquittal. The only exception was the Jewish Left, and even here there was much accommodation to the Zionist-inspired chauvinism prevalent in the wider Jewish community. This stands in sharp contrast to the reaction in non-Jewish circles and particularly of churches, with white congregations as well as Black, to the especially blatant frameup character of the case and to the exceptionally brutal persecution inflicted upon her.

True, the anger and resentment among Black people against their oppression and degradation have at times found expression in anti-Semitic utterances. But studies have shown that anti-Semitism is distinctly less pronounced among Black people than among whites. Furthermore, as a statement issued by the New York State Communist Party points out:

It is not the Black people who are the source of anti-Semitism. It is not they who are responsible for the flood of anti-Semitic filth which befouls the country. It is not they who are guilty of the economic and social discrimination against Jews which exists in our country.

In a word, it is not the Black people who are the oppressors of the Jews. On the contrary, it is the white power structure, including a small sector of Jewish capitalists, which maintains and benefits from the oppression of Black people.

To fail to see these things is to divert the very fight against anti-Semitism into a racist blind alley. It is to fall victim to those who would use the fraud of "Black anti-Semitism" as one more club against Black Americans. (*Daily World,* February 19, 1969.)

In a word, the fraud of "Black anti-Semitism" serves to align the Jewish people with the forces of reaction and to divert them from the struggle against their real enemies. And it has its roots in the false identification of Zionism with the interests of the Jewish people and the consequent equation of anti-Zionism with anti-Semitism.

It is Zionism, therefore, which is the central obstacle to any real struggle against anti-Semitism.

2. THE "JEWISH DEFENSE LEAGUE"

Shift to the Right

We have dealt above with the reactionary role of Zionism within the Jewish community. We have called attention specifically to the retreat of Jewish organizations and leaders from the fight against U.S. aggression in Indochina, to the general downgrading of the struggle against anti-Semitism, and to the rise of racism and the creation of the fictitious monster of "Black anti-Semitism" which has served to drive a wedge between the Jewish and Black peoples. And in the next chapter we shall deal at length with Zionism as the spearhead of anti-Sovietism in the United States.

In these respects and others, Zionism has behaved as an instrument of the ruling-class forces of reaction and racism in this country. And this role is but an expression of the reactionary, racist character of Zionism itself, which, as we have seen, leads it into ever greater subservience to U.S. imperialism. In particular, since the 1967 war there has taken place a pronounced shift to the Right among the Zionist forces.

In addition to the forms noted above, this finds expression in the development of ever closer ties of Zionist groups with Right-wing politicians, on the grounds that, whatever their stand on other questions, they are "friends of Israel." Among these "friends" is California's Governor Ronald Reagan, who not long ago was awarded a Medal of Valor by the Los Angeles Bonds for Israel Committee, with the presentation made by no less a person than Israeli Foreign Minister Abba Eban. In Philadelphia, B'nai B'rith presented a citizenship award to the ultra-racist Mayor Frank Rizzo. The Zionist Organization of America joined the procession by giving its Brandeis Award to Mayor Sam Yorty of Los Angeles. The chief speaker at the 62nd Annual Banquet of the Religious Zionists of America in June 1972 was Vice President Spiro Agnew. And so on.

At the celebration of the birth of Israel in New York's Carnegie Hall in April 1971, two of the main speakers were Senators Henry M. Jackson and James L. Buckley. Both are notorious Right-wing-ers and Buckley in the 1970 elections conducted one of the worst anti-Semitic campaigns by a major candidate in the history of the country. And the 1972 elections witnessed a major drive by Jewish leaders to swing Jewish voters into the Nixon camp.

Of course, this is not to say that all individuals or groups associated with Zionism follow an unrelieved course of support to reactionary views and policies. On the contrary, there are Jewish organizations and public figures that oppose the Indochina war. There are others who are disturbed by the rise in racism and the growing alliances with political reaction. Indeed, there is a rising opposition within Zionist circles which the Zionist Establishment, as we have seen, is doing its best to squelch. But this does not negate the fact that the basic thrust of Zionism within the Jewish community and the country as a whole is reactionary, and since 1967 increasingly so.

A Fascist Gang

The natural spawn of this reactionary trend is the so-called Jewish Defense League, embodying the extreme Right wing of Zionism. Originating in the mid-sixties as a vigilante group in Brooklyn, New York, ostensibly for the protection of Jewish residents from Black muggers, since 1968 it has blossomed forth under the leadership of the notorious Rabbi Meir Kahane in its present form—that of a gang of fascist hoodlums, of Jewish Brown Shirts.

As of late 1971, the JDL claimed a membership of some 14,000. In an interview with J. Anthony Lukas of *The New York Times Magazine* (November 21, 1971), Kahane stated:

In the [New York City] metropolitan area, we have 51 chapters, a little over 10,000 members, a little over 14,000 nationally. We have groups in Boston, Philadelphia, Miami, Chicago, Detroit, Cleveland, St. Louis, Houston, Albuquerque, Los Angeles and San Francisco. In Canada, we have them in Montreal and Toronto. In Europe we have them in London and Antwerp.

However, according to David A. Andelman *(The New York Times,* January 17, 1971), they concede "that they put on the membership list virtually anyone who sends them a sympathetic letter, much less the annual dues of $18 for an adult or $5 for a student. The

hard core of trained cadres, however, numbers only a few hundred."
But they involve substantial numbers of others in their activities, particularly groups of teen-age youth.

The Jewish people, according to the JDL, are in imminent danger of extinction, both in the Soviet Union and in the United States.

In the Soviet Union, Kahane maintains in his book *Never
Again!*, the Jews are in danger of physical extermination no less
than in Nazi Germany. He cries out: "There is no time! Another
holocaust could well approach!" The "saving" of Soviet Jews,
therefore, becomes the most urgent task before the JDL, and toward this end any action is justified. Its program calls for the cut-
ting off of all relations with the USSR, for relentless harassment of
Soviet personnel in the United States, for unceasing demonstrations
at Soviet offices, for sit-downs, chain-ins and other such acts.
In Kahane's words, the aim is nothing less than "to provoke a crisis
in U.S.-Soviet relations." That such a crisis brings with it a greatly
heightened danger of nuclear war seems to disturb Kahane and his
followers not in the least. Apparently, if nuclear war is required to
"liberate" the Soviet Jews, so be it.

U.S. Jews are also in grave danger. A JDL leaflet declares:

We are talking of JEWISH SURVIVAL!
Anti-Semitism is exploding in the United States.
Revolutionary Leftist groups—hostile to Israel and to Jewishness—are
*   capturing young people's minds and destroying law and order.*
Right-wing extremism is growing at an alarming rate.
Anti-Semitic Black racists are battling for control of the cities.

This is a central theme in Kahane's book. And in an article in *The
New York Times* (May 26, 1972) he states: "The first chapters
are beginning to emerge in what will be the most critical Jewish issue of the next decade—the physical survival of the largest community of Jews in the world, the Jews of the United States." The
prosperity of recent decades is fading, he says, and those who face
the loss of the good life they had enjoyed will "turn to demagogues
and racists who will promise them the good life in return for their
liberties and at the price of the scapegoat—the Jew. . . . What has
happened before can happen again and indeed, is beginning to happen already."

"The answer," he concludes, "is immediate mass emigration to

Israel. But failing this, Jews must organize to defend themselves, arms in hand if need be, from those who would destroy them."

It is not, however, Right-wing extremism which concerns the JDL. In their activities they pay precious little attention to the fascist ultra-Right. The chief threat to Jewish existence, they maintain, comes rather from another source. Says Kahane: "The most flagrant and dangerous incidents of Jew-hatred in our times have occurred and are occurring at the hands of the minority racial, mostly black, militants." *(Never Again!*, p. 99.)

Thus, according to the JDL, the threat to Jewish existence today comes from two main sources: the Black militants—those whom they designate as "anti-Semitic Black racists"—and the Soviet Union. And it has gone forth in typical gangster fashion to do battle against both. Its chief stock-in-trade has been anti-Sovietism, and its attacks have been centered on Soviet institutions, personnel and cultural events in this country, as well as on the Left here, particularly the Communist Party. But at the same time it has carried on a racist offensive against Black Americans.

Politically, the JDL has followed a generally Right-wing line. This is manifested particularly in its all-out support for the Indochina war. Kahane himself, in 1965, had joined with one Joseph Churba in authoring a book entitled *The Jewish Stake in Vietnam*. The JDL has also sought ties with reactionary or disreputable elements, such as its alliance with the reputed underworld figure Joseph A. Colombo, Sr., founder of the so-called Italian-American Civil Rights League. One of this organization's chief functions is to supply a respectable image for underworld leaders. It has also attracted the support of the notorious New Jersey racist Anthony Imperiale, among others. Further, on at least one occasion the JDL has conducted joint actions with the Young Americans for Freedom, the youth arm of the Birchites.

In pursuit of its aims the JDL has been guilty of a shocking series of outrages and crimes. Space forbids a cataloguing of these here, but by an admittedly incomplete count, the list as of February 1972 includes 14 bombings, 34 cases of assault and injury, 1 attempted hijacking, 11 instances of vandalism, 19 instances of rioting, 10 invasions of offices or meetings, 7 disruptions of cultural events, 15 cases of arms violations and about 1,200 arrests for disorderly conduct. (Rick Nagin, "A Force for Fascism," *World Magazine*, February 19, 1972.)

Most shocking are the bombings and attempted bombings, whose targets include the offices of the Palestine Liberation Organization, the New York Aeroflot office, the Soviet Embassy, the Iraqi UN Mission, the national headquarters of the Communist Party, the offices of the Soviet trade agency Amtorg, the Soviet UN Mission residence in Glen Cove, Long Island and the Washington headquarters of the Soviet news agency TASS. Each case was accompanied by anonymous telephone callers crying "Never Again"—the JDL slogan. Especially outrageous were the following incidents:

On October 20, 1971, four shots were fired from an adjacent roof into an eleventh-floor room of the Soviet UN Mission in New York in which four children were sleeping. Fortunately, none were hit.

On January 26, 1972 the offices of Sol Hurok Enterprises and Columbia Artists Management, Inc. in New York were firebombed. Both are agencies booking concerts for Soviet artists. In the Hurok offices a young Jewish woman was killed and 13 other individuals were injured.

As might be expected, the JDL has publicly denied responsibility for these crimes, though often applauding them. In the case of the Hurok and Columbia bombings, Kahane declared that these were the acts of "insane" people, while JDL vice president Bertram Zweibon attributed them to "provocateurs of the radical Left seeking to discredit the League." There is no doubt, however, that it is the JDL which is guilty of these criminal actions.

First of all, in May 1971 Kahane and six other JDL members were indicted in Federal Court in Brooklyn, New York, on charges of conspiring to transport a large arsenal of weapons across state lines and "to make, receive and possess explosive and incendiary devices." Subsequently Kahane and two other defendants pleaded guilty to the charge of conspiring to manufacture explosives, and considerable quantities of such explosives were afterward found. Kahane told newsmen that he and his followers would not be deterred from using explosives against Soviet facilities if they felt it necessary.

Secondly, in every case in which the culprits have been discovered, they have proven to be members of the JDL. In September 1971, seven JDL members were indicted on charges of conspiring to bomb the Amtorg offices and to plant a bomb at the Soviet Mission's Glen Cove estate. And in May 1972, four more JDL members were charged with plotting to bomb the Glen Cove estate during Nixon's visit to Moscow. In February 1972 a 17-year old youth described as a "former JDL activist" was arrested on charges of making a false statement in the purchase of the rifle used in the Soviet UN Mission shooting. And to cap it off, in June 1972, four JDL members were arrested on charges of bombing the Hurok and Columbia offices.

In November 1972, two of these indicted in the Glen Cove plot, who had pleaded guilty, were sentenced to prison terms of three years and a year and a day respectively. Other cases were still pending.

In addition to its anti-Soviet activities the JDL plays the role of a spearhead of extreme racism and chauvinism. Among its earliest claims to notoriety were its attacks on Black militants.

In May 1969, when James Forman, author of the *Black Manifesto,* announced that he would appear at Temple Emanu-El in New York to ask for reparations for Black people, a JDL gang lined up in front of the temple, armed with chains, sticks, pipes and baseball bats to prevent him from speaking. As it happened, Forman did not appear. Shortly afterward, when Muhammad Kenyatta spoke—by invitation—at the Main Line Temple in Philadelphia, a similar gang was on hand which, as he left, threatened him with violence should he ever return. Other exploits included an attempted attack on Black Panther headquarters in Harlem, and subsequently a physical assault by Kahane and a hundred of his goons on a group of Black students in the cafeteria of Brooklyn College. The alleged reason for this Nazi-like attack was that Black students had broken a Hebrew recording in the cafeteria juke box. At all times the JDL has done its utmost to sow dissension between Black and white and to create a lynch spirit against Black people.

The JDL's chauvinism is not confined to Black people, however; it extends equally to Arabs. Aside from the bombings of the Palestine Liberation Organization and the Iraqi UN Mission, in May 1970 three leaders of Arab organizations were severely beaten by groups armed with weighted clubs. Asked if the JDL took credit for the beatings, Kahane replied: "If we did we'd be open to all sorts of problems. You can quote me in exactly that manner." *(The New York Times,* May 23, 1970.)

Not even Jewish organizations are exempt from the JDL's gangsterism. In April 1971 a JDL mob forced its way into the offices of the New York Board of Rabbis and committed considerable damage. The reason, they said, was that the board had refused to provide bail for one Avraham Hershkovitz, a JDL official who was arrested with his wife at Kennedy Airport when they sought to board a London-bound United Arab Airlines plane with a grenade and four guns hidden in their clothing. According to authorities, they had planned to hijack an Arab airliner from London to Tel Aviv. Hershkovitz was sentenced to five years in prison for making false statements in his passport application. His wife jumped $15,000 bail and fled to Israel.

Hershkovitz was also one of the seven indicted for conspiring to bomb Amtorg. In January 1972 he pleaded guilty and was ordered deported to Israel upon completion of his prison term (evidently much abbreviated) in May. Apart from the comparative mildness of Hershkovitz's punishment, what is noteworthy is the way in which this case, in glaring contrast to that of the Soviet hijackers, has been hushed up by U.S. authorities, the communications media and the Jewish organizations. To this point we shall return later.

Such is the despicable crew which parades itself as "defenders" of the Jewish people. It has all the earmarks of a fascist gang—irresponsible warmongering, pathological anti-Communism and anti-Sovietism, extreme racism and chauvinism, and hoodlumism as a way of life. And its mentor, Kahane, is a fitting fuehrer for such a gang.*

Spawn of Zionism

The JDL is not some sort of fortuitous aberration. It is not an accidental development. On the contrary, it is the logical outgrowth of present-day Zionism and its increasingly reactionary trend. Its views

---

* For further details on the activities of the JDL and on the background of Kahane, see this author's pamphlet *The "Jewish Defense League"—A New Face for Reaction.*

are basically those of the "respectable"·Zionist organizations, carried to their extreme limits. Does the JDL advocate the removal of as many Soviet Jews as possible to Israel? So do the others; indeed, it is they who are leading the drive. Does the JDL inveigh against "Black anti-Semitism"? So do the others. Does the JDL fully support the expansionism of Israel's rulers? So do the others. And so on. The JDL's complaint is that the others do not conduct a real fight on these questions, and especially that they are derelict in the struggle to "save" Soviet Jews. It defends its own methods as being both necessary and effective.

The JDL, to be sure, has been strongly condemned by all major Jewish organizations and by many Jewish leaders. The Anti-Defamation League of B'nai B'rith has labeled it "a group of self-appointed vigilantes whose protection the Jewish community does not need or want." Rabbi Maurice N. Eisendrath referred to it as a collection of "goon squads" and compared it to the Ku Klux Klan. The New York Division of the American Jewish Congress called on U.S. Jews "to repudiate the lawlessness and self-defeating conduct of the Jewish Defense League." Many more statements of a similar character could be cited. What must be noted about all these statements, however, is that they condemn not the *aims* but only the *methods* of the JDL.* They reject the JDL's violence as morally wrong, and they maintain that its methods "will not bring one additional Jew out of the Soviet Union."

One would expect that an organization so clearly fascist in character and guilty of such heinous crimes as the JDL would not merely be condemned, but that the "respectable" Jewish elements would join in bringing these criminals to justice and putting this gang out of business. But no such thing has happened. Despite the verbal

---

* On one point disagreement does exist. Kahane's call for mass aliya on the grounds of a threat to Jewish existence here has, as one might expect, been widely rejected in leading Jewish circles, which strongly deny that any serious danger of anti-Semitism exists. Thus, in an article replying to Kahane (*The New York Times,* June 2, 1972) Morris B. Abram, honorary president of the American Jewish Committee, says: "No country, to my knowledge, has sustained individual liberty and group security at so high a level as has America during a period so beset with pressures. . . ." He adds: "The latest opinion polls show that since the end of World War II, there has been a dramatic decrease in anti-Semitism in the United States."

condemnations, there has been widespread toleration of the JDL. More, it enjoys a not inconsiderable body of sympathy in both Jewish and non-Jewish circles. On April 24 and 26, 1971 the Yiddish daily *Day-Jewish Journal* carried a by no means unfriendly interview with Kahane. At about the same time, *Look* published an article by its senior editor, Gerald Astor ("The Agonized American Jews," April 20, 1971), which treats Kahane and the JDL as a legitimate current in the Jewish community, on a par with the American Jewish Congress and the New Left.

Particularly significant are the events which took place at the international conference for the "liberation" of Soviet Jews held in Brussels in February 1971. Kahane appeared on the scene and asked to address the conference. He was refused admittance and was shortly afterward expelled from the country. But this, according to *The New York Times* of February 25, 1971, "threw the conference into an uproar, embarrassed its organizers and sharpened a split between a majority favoring peaceful pressure on the Soviet government and those who think that violence is necessary."

While Kahane has been refused permission to speak at their gatherings by most Jewish organizations, it is noteworthy that he was given the platform at the 1971 convention of the Zionist Organization of America. More recently, on March 20, 1971, he was guest speaker at the annual luncheon, held in New York, of the Jewish Teachers Association, an organization with some 30,000 members. The audience of 1,200, according to newspaper accounts, gave him a rising ovation and frequent bursts of applause.

The JDL has succeeded in establishing a base on a number of college campuses. At Brooklyn College it currently has a majority in the Student Council and is the dominant force on the campus, which it has virtually turned into its own private preserve.

Other examples could be given. But the foregoing are sufficient to make it clear that the JDL cannot be written off as an isolated handful of crackpots shunned by all decent people. On the contrary, it is a far greater menace than is indicated by the size of its membership. It has become an increasingly dangerous instrument of the forces of reaction, and there is reason to suspect that it operates as a direct tool of the CIA in its anti-Soviet intrigues. But it derives its main base from the fact that it is part of the Zionist movement, that it expresses in its own extreme fashion the views of Zionism. On all counts, it cannot be ignored.

Historical Roots

If the ideas of the JDL are not a mere isolated aberration, neither are they something new. The JDL has its historical roots in the Revisionist Party headed by Vladimir Jabotinsky, the original embodiment of the extreme Right wing of Zionism. This heritage is acknowledged by Kahane in his book. Jewish youth, he writes, should be taught about the great heroes of the Jewish people. And who are these heroes? None other than Jabotinsky and his most fanatical followers.

It was Jabotinsky's followers who in the days of the British Mandate organized the terrorist groups Irgun Zvai Leumi and the Stern gang, the former of which was responsible for the ghastly massacre of hundreds of Arab residents of the village of Deir Yassin in 1948. It is their tactics which serve as the model for the terrorist gangster methods of the JDL today.

The fascist character of Revisionism was evident long before these events. A. B. Magil writes:

It must also be admitted that long before the Irgun began bombing British police stations, the Revisionist gangs used bullets and bombs against the Jewish and Arab peoples of Palestine. Their youth group, Brit Trumpeldor (Betar for short), and specially organized goon squads broke strikes, bombed workers' clubs, and attacked meetings. Revisionist leaders developed a cult of violence whose resemblance to the tactics of Hitler and Mussolini could hardly have been accidental. In fact the Revisionists were at one time quite brazen about their ideological affinities. "Mussolini is the man who saved humanity from Communism," wrote one of them, who was tried in 1934 for membership in a secret terrorist band organized by his party. "We are the pioneers in the struggle against socialism, Marxism and Communism. For ten years we have been seeking a Jewish Mussolini. Help us find him." (Israel in Crisis, p. 120.)

Jabotinsky's own record of support to reaction goes back much further, to the days of his open collaboration with the Ukrainian White Guard pogromist Simon Petlura in the civil war following the October Revolution in Russia.

Today's heirs of Jabotinsky and the Revisionists are Menachem Begin and his ultra-Right Herut Party. Its youth organization, still called Betar, plays the same fascist hoodlum role in Israel that the JDL plays in this country. Betar, it may be noted, has a branch in the United States; in fact, it was as a member of this group that Kahane got his start.

The Revisionists and their successors have never been ostracized by the rest of the Zionist movement but have generally been an accepted part of it. Thus, Begin and his Right-wing Gahal group were represented in the Golda Meir government as part of the national coalition until mid-1970 when its representatives resigned in protest against the government's verbal assent to the U.S. initiative, which included an expression of readiness to implement UN Resolution 242. Jabotinsky himself, it is worth noting, is today viewed as a hero by all sections of the Zionists.

With these elements the JDL has close ties. Kahane himself commutes between the United States and Israel, where he is also engaged in organizing the JDL with at least the tacit approval of the Israeli authorities. Uzi Burstein writes in *Zo Haderekh,* organ of the Communist Party of Israel:

"The new world"—the rabbi Meir Kahane—has come to Israel, where during the last year a number of evident fascist organizations have sprung up, like mushrooms after rain. The arrival of the rabbi Kahane from the USA had been prepared by the establishment of organizations of the so-called "Jewish Defense League" in Israel and also by the establishment of additional fascist organizations, such as DB (Dikui-Bogdim, Hebrew for "suppression of traitors"). These organizations are mainly composed of members of Betar and of Herut. Their heroes are Menachem Begin and Ezer Weizman.

These organizations have set themselves the aim of creating a regime of terror and fear in Israel; to attack public meetings, demonstrations, clubs of any party or organization which opposes occupation and struggles for peace. The members of the fascist organizations are busy training in Judo, karate and methods of violence, wrapping their activities in a veil of mysticism of underground work, though the authorities and police do not impede their activities; on the contrary, they draw encouragement from the permissive attitude of police and the judicial bodies in this country, as happened at the trial against members of Betar who attacked the offices of the Communist Party of Israel, and as happens whenever they attack meetings and demonstrations of fighters for peace. (October 20, 1971.)

Thus the JDL has not only close ties with similar groups in Israel but also a base of toleration and support within Israeli ruling circles.

A Slap on the Wrist

The JDL has been repeatedly condemned by leading public officials, and on the occasion of each fresh outrage pledges have been made to put a stop to its criminal activities. Nevertheless, it has been able to carry on with relatively little hindrance. True, there have been numerous arrests and indictments. But the courts and other authorities have on the whole been remarkably lenient in these cases.

Kahane himself was twice convicted of comparatively minor offenses, suffering a fine of $500 in one instance and $250 in the other. In the more serious case, referred to above, of his indictment with others for conspiracy to transport arms across state lines and to manufacture explosives, a top-level deal said to involve the U.S. Attorney General's office permitted them to go free. Kahane and two other defendants pleaded guilty to the explosives charge. In return all charges against the others were dropped. The judge then proceeded to give the three individuals suspended sentences, place them on probation and fine them. Kahane received a five-year suspended sentence and probation period and was fined $5,000. The others received three-year suspended sentences and probation periods and lesser fines. The conditions of probation, as specified in the judge's written decision, included among others that "they may have nothing to do directly or indirectly with guns, bombs, dynamite, gunpowder, fuses, Molotov cocktails, clubs or any other weapons." But despite these conditions, Kahane has continued to be freely involved in the subsequent exploits of the JDL. And the other two were soon afterward indicted again, this time in connection with the attempted bombing of the Soviet Glen Cove residence.

Then there is the Hershkovitz case previously referred to. Guilty of two serious crimes he spent less than a year and a half in prison (apparently the longest period any JDL member has been imprisoned) and was then "deported" to Israel, to which his wife had already fled.

Courts have also been easy on JDL defendants in the matter of bail. The defendants in the Amtorg bombing, for example, were released on $10,000 personal bond (which meant that each had to put up 10 per cent or $1,000 in cash), with one exception who was released on his own recognizance. Even in the bombing of the Hurok offices, which involved actual murder, the bail was no more than $35,000.

The authorities, moreover, have done little to halt the anti-Soviet outrages of the JDL, despite repeated Soviet protests. In December 1970 the USSR found it necessary to cancel a projected visit to the United States of the Bolshoi opera and ballet companies because of "provocations perpetrated by Zionist extremists against Soviet institutions in the United States, as well as against Soviet artistic groups." In the following month a Soviet note was delivered to the U.S. ambassador in Moscow, calling attention to the persistent failure of U.S. authorities to protect Soviet facilities and personnel. In addition, the note charged that though the U.S. government had promised protection it was in fact "conniving at criminal actions" with the perpetrators of these provocations. And as late as May 1972 the Soviet Embassy in this country delivered a note to the State Department listing the numerous anti-Soviet acts of the JDL and requesting information on the steps taken to discover those guilty of them. As of a month later, no reply had been received.

To be sure, President Nixon has at times been impelled to express "regrets" and to make promises, and so has New York City's Mayor Lindsay. But in actual fact, government authorities have failed to take anything remotely approaching the measures required to curb Kahane and his fascist cohorts.

This failure, be it noted, stands in glaring contrast to the vindictive, murderous assaults on the Black Panthers and other Black militants, and to the trumped-up charges against them—charges of which juries later found them innocent. Furthermore, while Kahane and his friends have been permitted their freedom on low bail or personal recognizance, these Black victims of racial persecution have been held in prison for months and even years either without bail or—what amounts to the same thing—under astronomically high bail. Especially shocking is the contrast with the inhuman persecution of the heroic Black Communist woman Angela Davis, imprisoned without bail for some eighteen months, nearly all of it in solitary confinement, on a crude frame-up which literally fell apart in court.

Though glaring, the contrast is not surprising. From the extreme leniency toward the JDL one can only conclude that the Soviet government was fully justified in charging "connivance at criminal actions" with these elements. And indeed, the monopolist rulers of our country and their political spokesmen—notably the Nixons, Agnews, Reagans and their ilk—are not basically hostile to the JDL. On the contrary, they fully share its anti-Sovietism and racism. And they find such fascist gangs useful in the pursuit of their policies of aggression abroad and repression at home, just as the German monopolists once found Hitler's Brown Shirts useful. Hence the spectacle of the all-powerful U.S. government "unable" to protect the property or personnel of foreign governments in this country, or to curb the criminal conduct of a group of petty hoodlums.

To conclude, it is important to emphasize once more that the JDL is not an isolated aberration but is an integral part of the Zionist movement. Its own reactionary role derives from that of Zionism *as a whole,* not excluding its so-called "Left" or "socialist" sector. The JDL is but Zionism in its ugliest garb.

While others in the Zionist camp may sincerely repudiate it, therefore, they cannot do so on fundamental grounds but can only deplore its methods as reprehensible and harmful to a common cause. Above all, they are incapable of comprehending its essentially fascist character and of combatting it on these grounds. Hence, to conduct a serious struggle to put the JDL out of business it is necessary to fight against the reactionary trends within the Jewish community generally, which means that it is necessary to do battle against Zionism itself.

V

A SPEARHEAD OF ANTI-SOVIETISM

1. THE FRAUD "SOVIET ANTI-SEMITISM"

Zionism's Enmity Toward Socialism

If Zionism displays a lack of concern about anti-Semitism in the capitalist countries, it is utterly tireless in its crusading against alleged anti-Semitism in the Soviet Union and other socialist countries. The Zionists are driven to prove that anti-Semitism is indeed ineradicable and that it exists in socialist society no less—in fact, even more—than in capitalist society. They are imbued with a bitter enmity toward the socialist world for having removed the Jews living within its bounds from the Zionist orbit. It is an enmity which goes back to the October Revolution in 1917 and is directed first and foremost against the Soviet Union.

The Russian Zionists were bitterly hostile to the Bolsheviks. They opposed the October Revolution. In May 1918 a clandestine conference of Zeire Zion took place, which adopted a program to fight Communism. In the period of the civil war, Zionists took part in the counter-revolutionary governments of Denikin, Skoropadsky and Petlura, and established Zionist military units to fight with the White Guard forces. This enmity has never disappeared.

Zionists are totally blinded to the spectacular achievement of Soviet socialism in ending the degraded, poverty-stricken, pogrom-ridden ghetto existence of the Jewish people under tsarist oppression and elevating them to the status of Soviet citizens enjoying full equality with all others. They reject the fact that socialism, which eliminates the social basis of anti-Semitism, has effectively solved the Jewish question and has thereby removed all grounds for the existence of reactionary separatist movements.

Weizmann, in his memoirs, performs the remarkable feat of dealing with the entire period from 1917 to 1948 with virtually no mention of the Soviet Union other than some sorrowful references to the absence of Soviet Jews from Zionist world congresses. He makes no mention whatever of the role of the Soviet Union in saving untold Jewish lives from the Nazi butchers, in the establishment of the State of Israel or in supplying military aid to the newly born state to defend its independence. And he is totally silent on the liberation of the Soviet Jews from tsarist oppression.

To Ben-Gurion the wiping out of pogroms and ghettos and the integration of Soviet Jews into the life of their country seems little less than a calamity. In his address to the 25th World Zionist Congress in 1960 he speaks only of "the isolation and paralysis of Russian Jewry for the last forty years." He asserts that

. . . this Jewry has for forty years been condemned to silence and bereavement; its creative powers have been crushed by a foreign hand, its schools closed, its literature stifled and its authors led to execution, and an Iron Curtain has been erected between it and world Jewry, between it and the renascent homeland.

With the merits of these assertions we shall deal shortly. But the essence of Ben-Gurion's position is clear: oppression of Jews is no less under socialism than it was under tsarism.

Meir Kahane, fuehrer of the so-called Jewish Defense League, goes even farther. To him the cramped, ghettoized poverty-ridden life of the *shtetl*, with its religious medievalism, was a golden age of Jewry which the October Revolution destroyed.

Of the saving of Jews from the Hitlerites, Ben-Gurion has only this to say:

Only one Jewish community in Nazi-occupied Europe was saved from Hitler's hangmen—that of Bulgaria, when the Bulgarian king told the Nazi conqueror that the Jewish people would be destroyed only over his dead body.* This exception casts a heavy and terrible load of

* Ben-Gurion is entirely wrong on this point. It was not the intervention of the pro-fascist king which saved the Bulgarian Jews but the struggles of workers and other sections of the people—and of the Jews themselves— largely led by the Bulgarian Communists. The documents of this heroic struggle are published in the 1971 *Annual* of the Social, Cultural and Educational Association of the Jews in the People's Republic of Bulgaria.

guilt on Hitler's other allies, who could have saved the Jews if they had wanted.

The implications of this statement are frightening. Ben-Gurion's complaint is not that these others were allies of Hitler; it is only that they did nothing to save Jews. One is reminded of those German Jews who were fully prepared to support Hitler if only he would abandon his anti-Semitism. But twenty million Soviet citizens, among them Soviet Jews, gave up their lives to defeat fascism and to save the lives of Jews everywhere in the world, including Palestine. In the view of Ben-Gurion, this never happened.

According to Amos Elon, in his book *The Israelis: Founders and Sons,* this falsification of history is general. "When Israeli historians reflect upon events prior to and during World War II," he writes, "they invariably conclude that, during this greatest calamity that has befallen the Jewish people in their long history, few non-Jews and no single sovereign state had actually come to their rescue with a specific intention to save them" (p. 277).

Such is the overpowering hatred of the Soviet Union and socialism in these Zionist circles. True, there were at one time other, Leftward-leaning sectors of the Zionist movement which took a more positive attitude toward the Soviet Union. But these, never more than a small minority, have long ago joined the anti-Soviet pack. And not surprisingly, for this is the logic of Zionism.

The Anti-Soviet Crusade

Zionist hostility toward the Soviet Union reached new extremes with the 1967 war. Since then there has developed an anti-Soviet drive unprecedented in its ferocity.

On the one hand the Soviet Union is charged with supporting those forces which seek the destruction of the State of Israel, and with arming the Arab states for that purpose. In his speech to the Biennial Convention of the American Jewish Congress in 1970, its president Rabbi Arthur J. Lelyveld spoke of "the increasing boldness of Soviet intervention to give direct support to the Arab threat to Israel's existence." Avraham Avidar, Minister of Information of the Israeli Embassy, declared in his address to the Convention: "Soviet imperialism is today the single most important factor blocking the road to peace in the Middle East." He added: "The world must know, Russia must know that Israel will not be another Czechoslovakia." (*Congress Bi-Weekly,* June 19, 1970.)

Ira Hirschmann, in his book *Red Star over Bethlehem,* states:

> The Soviet leaders know that the United States, regardless of the extent of American economic and sympathetic ties with the Arab states, cannot in good conscience or in good politics support a policy aimed at eradication of the State of Israel or any other independent state. Genocide can never become an instrument of American political policy, but it is a fair assumption that it is a tactic from which the Kremlin would not flinch if it suited their purpose (p. 44).

Mr. Hirschmann is apparently unaware of what has been happening in Indochina. But we shall return to his "fair assumption" below.

On the other hand the Soviet Union is accused of the most inhuman persecution of its Jewish citizens, of forcibly depriving them of their religious and cultural rights, of grossly discriminating against them in employment and education, of preventing them from migrating to Israel where they can "live as Jews," and of a host of other abuses. Soviet Jews are said to be living in fear and terror. The "liberal" American Jewish Congress speaks of nothing less than the "Soviet inquisition of Jews." (*Congress Bi-Weekly,* January 22, 1971.) Indeed, not a few of the accusers go as far as to liken the lot of Soviet Jews to that of the Jews under Hitler, and to speak of genocide.

So hysterical and divorced from reality have these charges become that even spokesmen who are by no means pro-Soviet have been impelled to caution against going to such extremes. C. L. Sulzberger, in a *New York Times* column datelined Moscow (July 1, 1970), states that "the regime itself is not committed to internal anti-Semitism" and that "real anti-Semitism is concentrated among relatively few bigots." *The New York Times* Moscow correspondent Bernard Gwertzman writes (December 27, 1970): "There is certainly no wave of officially-inspired anti-Semitism sweeping the Soviet Union" (though there are, he says, individual instances of anti-Semitism). Nahum Goldmann has repeatedly noted that Soviet Jews enjoy equal civil rights with all other Soviet citizens and has warned against distortions on this point. And Dr. William Korey of B'nai B'rith, according to the *New York Post* (December 29, 1970), "admits that there has been little overt anti-Semitism—no public accusations that Russian Jews are in league with Israel, and no internal publicity about the current Leningrad trials."

More recently such cautions have come from no less a source than the State Department itself. They were voiced by Richard T. Davies, Deputy Assistant Secretary for European Affairs, before a House Foreign Affairs Committee subcommittee investigating "denial of rights to Soviet Jews." He said:

. . . there can be no comparison with the terrible era of the Nazi holocaust or Stalin's blood purge of Jewish intellectuals. With respect to the majority, claims that Soviet Jews as a community are living in a state of terror seems to be overdrawn. Jews continue to be eminent in the Soviet economic, journalistic, scientific, medical and cultural worlds, in numbers far out of proportion to their percentage of the population. They are still the best educated Soviet minority. There is little evidence that the regime's "anti-Zionist" propaganda has spilled over into outright and widespread anti-Semitism or deliberate and sustained efforts to fan a "pogrom" mentality in Soviet society at large. *(Hearings before the Subcommittee on Europe,* p. 40.)

Nevertheless, the anti-Soviet campaign goes on full blast. At its center is the American Jewish Conference on Soviet Jewry, sponsored by a number of prominent Jewish organizations. It is accompanied by the Academic Committee on Soviet Jewry, headed by the indefatigable Hans J. Morgenthau. A well-financed institution called Jewish Minorities Research pours out ream upon ream of slick propaganda on the alleged plight of Soviet Jews. And the leading Jewish organizations have made this question the number one point on their agendas.

This ill-begotten crusade is not a recent development; on the contrary, it is one of many years' standing. It had its chief origins in extreme Right-wing circles and in the State Department. Prominent among its earlier champions was the late Senator Thomas J. Dodd, notorious for his anti-Communism and anti-Sovietism, and later censured by the Senate for his financial irregularities. In an article in *U.S. News and World Report* ("The Hotbed of Anti-Semitism —It's Soviet Russia, Not Germany," March 28, 1960), he said: "Between the brutality of Soviet anti-Semitism and the brutality of Nazi anti-Semitism, there is little to choose. About all that is lacking so far is the gas chambers."

Another such "friend" of the Soviet Jews was the Hearst press. Scarcely distinguished as a champion of the Jews when they were being exterminated by Hitler and long a mouthpiece for the pro-fascist rantings of a Westbrook Pegler, it has come forward as a self-styled defender of Soviet Jewry. A series of articles by one Leslie L. Whitten in 1964 spoke of the Soviet Jews as living under "unrelenting terror." Referring to bloody religious persecutions of past centuries, Whitten wrote: "Imagine that only 20 years ago such a bloodbath had drowned your brethren and imagine that already now, today, the specter of more such horror was abroad in the land. That is what it is to be a Jew today in Russia." (*New York Journal American,* May 5, 1964.)

Such elements as these, racist and anti-Semitic to the core, obviously have no concern whatever for the welfare of Soviet Jews; their only aim is to undermine the Soviet Union in every way possible and to sharpen U.S.-Soviet tensions. It is in such company that the leading Jewish organizations have placed themselves. And they have attracted other strange allies such as Russian Whiteguard emigré groups and pogromist Ukrainian nationalists.

Since 1967 the activities of these Jewish organizations have been tremendously stepped up. There has been a flood without precedent of public meetings, mass demonstrations, picket lines, petition campaigns, full-page newspaper advertisements and similar actions. These, it must be noted, represent no spontaneous outpouring of the Jewish masses. On the contrary, they are highly organized, well-financed and extremely well-publicized operations, depending primarily on the participation of captive groups such as the student bodies of Jewish parochial schools.

Under the spurious slogan "Let my people go," they focus on the demand for the migration of Soviet Jews *en masse* to Israel. U.S. Zionists, who themselves have not the remotest intention of going to live in Israel, are leading the call for a great "ingathering of the exiles"—from the Soviet Union. At the center of this drive are the Israeli Zionist ruling circles, searching for mass Jewish immigration to populate the occupied territories which they hope to incorporate into the State of Israel.

The most important problem, the late Premier Levi Eshkol told a study mission of the United Jewish Appeal from the United States in October 1967, is the need for a rapid and substantial rise in the number of Jews in Israel. He said: "We must make sure of a large aliya to Israel. You know the problems involved: you know where the Jews are who want to come to Israel, but can't; and where the Jews are who can come, but don't." (*Jerusalem Post,* October 30, 1967.) In its report to the 27th World Zionist Congress in 1968, the Jewish Agency was more explicit, expressing its concern over "how to populate with Jews the newly liberated areas" in the face of a general slowing down of immigration.

The zeal displayed by leading Zionist circles in this unholy crusade stands in striking contrast to their extreme reticence to act against manifestations of anti-Semitism here or even, at the time, against the unspeakable Hitler atrocities. They are primarily moved, it is clear, not by a concern with fighting anti-Semitism but by anti-Sovietism and a passion for bringing Soviet Jews to Israel.

The Big Lie

The basis of this campaign, as we have noted, is the fiction that life for Jews in the Soviet Union has been rendered intolerable. It is impossible, within the confines of this small volume, even to catalogue the accusations levelled against the Soviet Union, let alone answer them. Here we can do no more than to select some of the more glaring examples of falsification in order to illustrate the character of the campaign as a whole. Toward this end, let us examine some of the allegations contained in a "Fact Sheet on Anti-Jewish Discrimination" published by the American Jewish Congress (*Congress Bi-Weekly,* March 19, 1971).

The "Fact Sheet" states: "The number of Jewish students in secondary schools remained constant at 47,000 from 1962–63 to 1967, compared to an increase of students of Ukrainian nationality of 154 per cent, Uzbeks 198 per cent and other nationality groups amounting to more than 100 per cent." But according to the USSR Central Statistics Board, the number of Jewish college students in the academic year 1962–63 was 79,300 and in 1968–69 111,900—an increase of more than 40 per cent. And this although the Soviet Census records a decline in the Jewish population in this period. The statistics show that 3.15 per cent of the Jewish population are college students, compared to 1.82 per cent of the total population. Perhaps the AJC has more reliable sources; if so, they are not disclosed.

In any event, this is scarcely evidence of the imposition of a quota system on Jewish students. And if the enrollment of Jews as a percentage of total college enrollment has decreased over the past few decades, this is readily explained by the relatively greater rise in college attendance by students of other nationalities, many of which lived in almost total illiteracy in tsarist days. Yet this hoary lie continues to be diligently propagated by "respectable" Jewish organizations and spokesmen.

The evidence offered is that among Jews, overwhelmingly concentrated in urban centers, the proportion of young people seeking higher education is greater than among other nationalities. But *how much* greater? The proportion of Jewish enrollment in higher educational institutions is 70 per cent above the national average. Is the proportion seeking admission higher than this? To this question no answer is given.

The "Fact Sheet" states further: "Although Jews continue to play an important role in Soviet science, the percentage of Jewish scientific research personnel has dropped steadily from 16.8 per cent in 1947 to 11 per cent in 1955 to 7.7 per cent in 1967." This is intended to give the impression that Jews are being progressively displaced from this field. But the number of Jews engaged in scientific research, according to the USSR Central Statistics Board, rose from 29,000 in 1958 to nearly 61,000 in 1968. Jews comprise the third-greatest number of research workers, exceeded only by Russians and Ukrainians, though they constitute only about one per cent of the USSR's population. Moreover, of 278 recipients of the Lenin prize on the occasion of the anniversary of the October Revolution in 1971, 39 (or 14 per cent) were Jews. Of 81 recipients in the field of science, seven were Jews, and they numbered 29 of 160 winners in technology.

Again, this is hardly evidence of anti-Jewish discrimination. And here, too, if Jews have declined as a percentage of the total, this can readily be explained by the relatively greater entry of other national groups into this field of work.

The "Fact Sheet" asserts: "Jews are totally excluded from Soviet military academies and training schools for diplomats. Others go further. William Korey of B'nai B'rith states: "Certain areas of activity are *Judenrein*, e. g., the diplomatic corps." (*Hearings before the Subcommittee on Europe*, p. 142.) And a fact sheet issued by the American Jewish Conference on Soviet Jewry some years ago alleges that "Jews have virtually disappeared from key 'security-sensitive' areas such as the armed forces, diplomatic corps and membership in the Supreme Soviets of the 15 republics."

Let us note, first of all, that among the top-ranking officers in the Soviet army are General Yakov Kreizer, Colonel-Generals David Dragunsky and Alexander Tsirlin, Major-Generals Zinovy Kontsevoi and Lev Dovator, and Lieutenant-Generals Matvei Vainraub, Shimon Krivoshein and Grigory Plaskov—all Jews. In the lower ranks the number of Jewish officers is much higher. The Soviet diplomatic corps includes at least two top diplomats who are Jewish: N. Tsarapkin and G. Mendelevich.

We have no statistics on Jewish and non-Jewish enrollment in military academies or schools for diplomats (and the compilers of the "Fact Sheet" do not divulge the source of their information). It is interesting to note, however, that the head of a leading military academy is none other than General David Dragunsky.

Some 8,000 Jews are deputies to Soviets at all levels. There are at least five Jewish deputies in the Supreme Soviet. A number of Jews hold important administrative posts, among them Veniamin Dymshitz, Deputy Chairman of the Council of Ministers of the USSR; Semyon Ginsburg, Chairman of the Board of the Construction Bank of the USSR; Lev Volodarsky, Deputy Chairman of the Central Board of Statistics of the USSR; Yuli Bokserman, Deputy Minister of the Gas Industry of the USSR; Iosif Ravich, Deputy Minister of Communications of the USSR; and numerous others. (See *Jews in the USSR,* pp. 50–51.)

The French-Jewish leader Andre Blumel, who recently visited Uzbekistan, reports: "There are three or four vice-ministers and the chief of the cabinet of the president of the Supreme Soviet of Uzbekistan is a Jew." (Interview in *Naie Presse,* February 2 and 3, 1971.) Undoubtedly this situation is duplicated in other republics.

It is true that the number of Jews holding public office has declined over the past number of years. But it can hardly be said that they have "virtually disappeared" from this field.

Jewish Culture in the USSR

At the very heart of these accusations is the charge that the Soviet government pursues a deliberate policy of obliterating Jewish culture and religion—a policy of "cultural genocide" in relation to Jews.

Thus, the "Fact Sheet" states:

> Today there is not one single school or classroom in the Soviet Union where Jewish culture and history are taught, either in Yiddish, Hebrew or Russian. This is so even though 500,000 Jews declared Yiddish to be their mother tongue in the 1959 census and the Soviet Constitution grants every group of 20 parents the right to have their children educated in their mother tongue.*

Others go beyond this, charging that the teaching of Yiddish or Hebrew is not only not provided for but is forbidden. A letter to *The New York Times* (December 30, 1970), signed by such prominent figures as Theodore M. Hesburgh, Arthur Miller, Hans J. Morgenthau, Bayard Rustin, Telford Taylor and others, speaks of a "nationally concerted secret police action aimed at militant Jews who have . . . secretly dared to study Jewish history and the Hebrew language." A "fact sheet" authored by Richard Maass, chairman of the American Jewish Conference on Soviet Jewry, states: "The only place Hebrew is taught in the Soviet Union is in a Russian Orthodox seminary." (*Hearings before the Subcommittee on Europe*, p. 208.) The renegade Mikhail Zand, in a lecture at Columbia University on October 6, 1971, claimed that after 1928 "all Hebrew literary activity in the Soviet Union was forbidden."

Such notions are widely propagated. But they are false.

At Leningrad University, according to the late Soviet journalist Solomon Rabinovich:

---

* In the 1970 census about 381,000, or 17.7 per cent of the total Jewish population, declared Yiddish to be their mother tongue, compared to 20 per cent in 1959.

A very important course of lectures is delivered by Professor Isaac Vinnikov, the universally acknowledged head of the Leningrad School of Semitologists and Hebraists, a linguist and ethnographer of world importance, an expert on the Hebrew, Aramaic, Syrian, Phoenician, Ungaritic and Arabic languages. His lectures on Biblical texts always evoke great interest. Recently, on Professor Vinnikov's initiative, a course in modern spoken Hebrew was included in the curriculum.

Isaac Vinnikov's pupil, Gita Gluskina, teaches Hebrew grammar at the University and with the students reads Biblical texts containing folklore and also historical and philosophical treatises. Under her guidance students learn to appreciate the beauty of the medieval poetry of Yehuda Halevi, Moses ibn Ezra and Solomon ibn Gabirol and acquaint themselves with the fundamentals of Jewish poetry. *(Jews in the Soviet Union,* p. 78.)

In addition, a Russian-Hebrew dictionary has been published and its counterpart, a Hebrew-Russian dictionary, is at this writing in preparation.

Nor is this confined to Leningrad. The Israeli sociologist Haim Darin-Drabkin reports the following concerning his visit to the Lenin Library in Moscow some years ago:

In answer to my question as to whether there was a special Hebrew language section in the Oriental Languages Department, the astonishing reply came that there was indeed such a section, but that it was in the Department of Languages of the Soviet Peoples. I asked why and was told that the Jewish minority of the Soviet Union has two languages—Yiddish and Hebrew—and I should look, therefore, for the Hebrew section in the building where books of the national minorities are to be found. I expected to find only Hebrew classics, but was pleasantly surprised to find that even contemporary Israeli authors of my own acquaintance are represented on the shelves. The librarian in charge of this section, however, complained that few readers visited it. The library had organized Hebrew courses, she told me. ("Encounters with Jews in the USSR," *Israel Horizons,* May 1964.)

There is an Oriental Department at Tbilisi University in Georgia. One of its students, Isaak Davitashvili, is described by the Soviet journalist S. Novich as "an expert on ancient Jewish literature. He has translated into the Georgian many masterpieces of Jewish classics, including books by Judah Halevi, Shelomo ibn Gabirol, Moses ibn Ezra, Immanuel of Rome and others." Davitashvili said that he planned to specialize in Jewish historiography. *(In a Close-Knit Family of Nations,* p. 59.)

And these few examples by no means exhaust the list.

Yet we are asked to believe that "militant Jews" were compelled to conduct secret classes in Hebrew! And more, that they were punished for doing so!

Nor are Soviet Jews prohibited from studying Yiddish or Jewish history. It is true that there are no Jewish schools in the Soviet Union. But this is not because they are banned; on the contrary, it is because Soviet Jews themselves do not want such schools. Riva Vishchinikina, chairman of the Executive Committee of the Valdheim Rural Soviet of the Jewish Autonomous Region, states:

> Although I, in my day, attended a Jewish school, I sent my children to a Russian one. Why? Well, judge for yourself. Besides Jews in our village of Valdheim there are Russians, Ukrainians, Byelorussians, Tatars and Bashkirs. The children play together, are brought up together in the kindergarten, make friends. It would be cruel to separate them from each other, isolate them. Wouldn't sending them to a Jewish school, when all the rest of the children of other nationalities are studying together in a Russian school, isolate and hurt them irreparably?
>
> But I didn't send my children to a Jewish school because of one other, no less important, reason. On finishing a Russian school, they will be able to continue their education in Khabarovsk, Moscow, Leningrad or any other big city—in other words, in the educational institutions of large centers, which have absorbed the very best of Russian and foreign scientific thought. Those are the lines along which not only Jewish mothers reason, but Tatar, Armenian, Uzbek and others living in the Russian Federation. It may sound paradoxical, but it is a fact: Jewish mothers closed the Jewish schools. However, all those who wish to learn Yiddish can study it at home, privately, or in courses, or by joining amateur Jewish theatrical groups. The monthly magazine *Sovetisch Heimland* has Yiddish lessons in every issue. (*Soviet Life,* July 1971.)

In the early days of the Soviet Union, when Jews were still living in compact ghetto communities and most Jewish children knew only Yiddish, a network of schools taught in Yiddish was established. But with freedom to live and work anywhere and to attend Russian schools—a cherished but usually unattainable dream of Jewish parents in tsarist days—these schools eventually found themselves without students. The simple fact, as Vishchinikina makes clear, is that Soviet Jews do not want their children segregated into separate Jewish schools. Nor do the children want it.

As for classes in Yiddish, these are neither banned nor non-existent. Although the Soviet Constitution contains no such provision as the AJC "Fact Sheet" claims, official assistance is available to any group which wishes to organize such classes. For example, Soviet news sources reported in early 1971 that special courses in Yiddish had been organized in Leningrad by a group of parents. The authorities had aided them in getting teachers and classrooms, for which they paid a nominal fee.

Not surprisingly, the demand for Yiddish classes is small. Certainly those who claim Yiddish as their mother tongue (overwhelmingly older people) are scarcely in need of classes in it. And just as in the United States, the younger generation has little interest in learning Yiddish. To those who bewail the absence of Yiddish education it should be pointed out that in this country secular Yiddish schools are virtually non-existent.

The suppression of Yiddish in the USSR, it is maintained, is demonstrated also by the relatively small number of books published in that language. According to the AJC "Fact Sheet," between 1960 and 1968 there were only eight. It admits that the number has increased since then but adds: "Those books published since 1969 have been almost exclusively reprints of earlier volumes rather than original works. Moreover, they have been distributed in large part abroad—to serve Soviet propaganda purposes rather than Yiddish readers in the Soviet Union."

But this misrepresents the facts. Between 1965 and 1970 no less than 30 books in Yiddish were published, many of them new works by present-day writers. And they can be obtained in Moscow as well as in New York. Moreover, these critics ignore the question of the *quality* of what is published, not only in these books but in the voluminous output of *Sovetisch Heimland,* a monthly literary journal with a circulation of some 25,000 and with a reputation for high literary standards. In its ten years of existence it has introduced the works of more than a hundred Yiddish writers. And it has held numerous readers' conferences which discussed literary matters among other subjects.

On the trend in Soviet Yiddish literature, Joel Cang wrote in 1966:

The stream of Jewish literature in Soviet Russia is widening. Since its re-emergence as a vehicle of literary expression some five years ago,

Yiddish has succeeded in reasserting itself and winning due recognition both at home and abroad. Allowing for the limitations which a rigid adherence to socialist realism imposes on Jewish, as well as other creative art in Communist Russia, the Yiddish novelists and poets in the USSR are making a solid contribution to the mainstream of Jewish writings of our time. ("Is There a Revival of Jewish Literature in Russia?," condensed from *The Jewish Quarterly* in *Jewish Digest,* December 1966.)

Can it be said that the stream of Yiddish literature is widening in the United States? Or in Israel? Hardly. Yet there is no end to irresponsible charges that it is being throttled in the Soviet Union.

Even more important is the fact that books by Jewish writers are widely translated into Russian, Ukrainian and other languages. Between 1955 and 1969, 466 such books were published in editions totalling more than 46 million copies. Among these are the complete works of the great classical writers Sholem Aleichem, Y. L. Peretz and Mendele Mocher Sforim, who are known and read throughout the Soviet Union, as well as the writings of many Soviet novelists and poets. Yet these facts, indicative of the high esteem in which Jewish literature is held by Soviet citizens of all nationalities and not merely the relative few who read Yiddish, are totally ignored. It may be added that the Union of Soviet Writers, in a membership of some 7,100, includes 835 Jewish writers, or about 12 per cent of the total.

As for the United States, a look at the latest edition of *Books in Print* discloses that while a number of Sholem Aleichem's writings are available in English, there are only three books by Peretz and Mocher Sforim listed. And on the centenary of Sholem Aleichem's birth some years ago, two countries issued a commemorative stamp to mark the occasion: Israel and the Soviet Union. There is a plaque on the house in which he lived in Kiev, and streets in Kiev and other cities and towns are named after him. No such regard for his memory has been shown in the United States, though he spent his last years here.

The Soviet critics complain of the absence of Yiddish newspapers in the Soviet Union. But there does exist a Yiddish newspaper—the *Birobidjaner Shtern,* published five times a week and circulating far beyond the confines of Birobidjan. In other words, such newspapers are not forbidden.

With regard to the Yiddish theater the "Fact Sheet" states that in contrast to the numerous Yiddish theaters of past years, "Today there is not one full-time theatrical group. Instead, there are local part-time traveling theatrical companies in Vilna, Birobidjan and Kishinev whose success before Jewish audiences (an estimated 500,000 spectators per year) testify to the yearning for Jewish culture and art among the Jews of the USSR."

Here again the picture is falsified. In Moscow one finds a drama company directed by Veniamin Shvartser, a musical comedy group headed by Anna Guzik and a company of five led by Sidi Tal, which does musical skits and dramatic sketches. These are *professional* groups and they perform not only in Moscow but in other parts of the USSR as well. And there are amateur dramatic groups not only in Vilna, Birobidjan and Kishinev, but also in Leningrad, Kaunas, Tallinn and other cities. In addition there are many recitations of Yiddish stories and poems, as well as concerts of Jewish songs.

To be sure, this falls considerably short of what existed some decades ago. But in the United States, where the Yiddish theater was once a flourishing institution, today it is moribund, and almost no serious Yiddish drama is produced. The Polish actress Ida Kaminska, who left Poland hoping to find greener pastures here, finds herself instead with no theater and with no prospects beyond an occasional production of a play when financial backing can be found. In Israel there is no Yiddish theater worthy of the name. By comparison, Soviet Jews enjoy greater, not less access to Yiddish theater.

Religious Freedom of Soviet Jews

It is also alleged that Soviet Jews are severely restricted in their ability to practice their religion, that there are few synagogues and even these are being arbitrarily shut down, that no seminary exists, that prayer books and other religious objects are unobtainable, as are kosher foods. Of all these things, it is charged, Soviet Jews are being deliberately deprived by the Soviet government.

Thus, the AJC "Fact Sheet" complains:

In 1956 there were 450 synagogues in the USSR. In 1969 this figure has been reduced to 55—this despite the Soviet law that grants believers the right to form religious societies and to have religious buildings constructed for the purpose of prayer and worship. There are only three functioning rabbis in the USSR today, two of them more than 75 years old. . . . Jews are prohibited from manufacturing phylacteries, prayer shawls and other articles required for Jewish worship. Kosher meat is unobtainable in the Soviet Union.

Lewis Feuer, in an article which reaches rock bottom for falsification and slander, states: "They have no kosher food; if somebody secretly sells a kosher chicken, there is a prison-term." ("Soviet Marranos," *Judaism,* Winter 1964, reprinted in *Jewish Digest,* July 1970.)

But these allegations are no less false than the others. The fact is that those Jews who wish to practice their religion are perfectly free to do so. Any group of 20 or more may establish a synagogue, and any group of 10 or more may form a minyan, conducting religious services in members' homes or in other places. There are today nearly 100 synagogues and 300 minyanim in the Soviet Union. (The latter are never mentioned by the anti-Soviet detractors. Neither is the fact that the figure of 450 for 1956 also includes minyanim.)

It is true that over the past few decades the number of Jewish congregations has appreciably decreased. But this is not peculiar to the Jewish religion; the number of Russian Orthodox churches has shown a corresponding decline. It is due not to administrative closing down of synagogues or churches but to a drastic drop in the number of religious practitioners. According to Soviet sociologists, the number of Jewish believers is very small, ranging from 3–6 per cent in the Russian Federation and the Ukraine to 7–12 per cent in Georgia, the Northern Caucasus and Bukhara. And they are mostly old people. It is worth noting that in Georgia, where the proportion of believers is highest, there are 16 synagogues for a total population of some 50,000 Jews. In other words, where they are wanted they are available.

The late Rabbi Yehuda Leib Levin of Moscow, in an address delivered during his visit to this country in 1968, stated:

The doors of our Moscow Great Synagogue, from the time of the Revolution to the present day, have been open to all worshippers and all visitors . . . and prayers are conducted there during the day, the

Talmud is studied there, and the Mishnah, the Shulchan Aruch and the Chumosh. There is available a slaughterhouse for poultry, a ritual bath, and those who perform circumcisions. The Community Council provides Jews with matzoh, not only for Moscow Jews but also for Jews of other places. ("A Soviet Rabbi Speaks to American Jewry," *New World Review,* Summer 1968.)

Two Georgian correspondents of *Soviet Weekly* report (March 21, 1970) that in the city of Kutaisi, where there are three synagogues, "there are kosher slaughterhouses, and both the Great and Small synagogues have their own bakeries for Matzoh. There are eight butchers selling kosher meat, a Jewish bath-house and a Jewish cemetery."

A religious calendar is published yearly by the Moscow Central Synagogue, and in 1968 a new prayer book edited by Rabbi Levin was issued in 10,000 copies. It should be noted that in the Soviet Union there is complete separation of church and state and that religious institutions must provide for themselves. But they are in no way *prohibited* from doing so, and this applies to Jews as well as Christians and Mohammedans.

It is not true that "there are only three functioning rabbis in the USSR today." In Georgia alone there are at least five times this number. Moreover, a conference of representatives of Jewish religious communities, held in Moscow in March 1971, numbered ten rabbis from other parts of the Soviet Union among the members of its leading committees and its published speakers. And this is by no means the total number. Certainly the number of rabbis in the Soviet Union is far smaller than that in the United States, and certainly it is decreasing as the number of Jewish congregations decreases. But it is also certain that the "Fact Sheet" falsifies the picture.

Nor is it true that no Jewish seminary is available in the USSR. Rabbi Levin, in the above-cited speech, reported that in 1956 a Yeshiva was opened in Moscow with the consent of the government, but he added that "the youth have completely removed themslves from Judaism so that students for the Yeshiva are very difficult to find." And indeed, there have been very few candidates. According to the London *Jewish Chronicle* (March 24, 1972), the Yeshiva, though closed for a time, was currently in operation, with an enrollment expected to reach 25.

The fact is that, like other religions, Judaism is dying out in the Soviet Union. Religion is declining also in the United States; the difference is that in the Soviet Union there is no major social force operating to keep it alive. On the contrary, religious belief is discouraged as being anti-scientific and a mark of backwardness, hence its much more rapid decline. But this is true of *all* religion, and the low estate of Judaism is no proof whatever of a policy of discrimination against Jews.

It is only those who identify Jewish life with Judaism who find in these developments a monstrous plot of the Soviet government to destroy Jewish identity. Least of all do the overwhelming majority of Soviet Jews see the matter in this light. Aaron Vergelis, editor of *Sovetisch Heimland,* puts it in these words:

> We live in a country where more than half a century ago the old order was abolished. We have a different way of life. It corresponds to our convictions. We believe that the Jewish people must go forward on the road of the twentieth century.
>
> They maintain that Jews will be able to preserve their identity only if they attend synagogue regularly, remain captive to tradition, and return to the usages of past centuries. They say that if we follow new paths, we are no longer Jews. We, on the contrary, are convinced that we are Jews only when we live in a new way and are part of new times. (*Daily World Magazine,* April 18, 1970.)

A Non-Existent "Official Policy"

The various types of alleged anti-Jewish discrimination discussed in the foregoing pages, it is maintained, stem from an official policy of anti-Semitism on the part of the Soviet government. One "proof" offered of the existence of such a policy is the appearance of books, articles or cartoons with anti-Semitic content or overtones. Hans J. Morgenthau, in a letter to *The New York Times* (July 7, 1970), contends that "in view of the totalitarian control of printed publications in the Soviet Union," the appearance of such writings and cartoons indicates government approval. "If the government were not in favor of such publications," he says, "they would not be published."

But Morgenthau and his fellow critics have an erroneous idea of how things get published in the Soviet Union, arising from their mistaken conception of socialist society as "totalitarian." Take the case of book publication. There is no all-knowing, all-powerful board of censors, passing on all books submitted for publication. On the contrary, each of the numerous institutions involved in book publication makes its own determinations. Manuscripts are submitted for critical reading to people considered competent in the given field, and acceptance or rejection is based on their recommendations.

To illustrate the point, in an interview with Samuel Zivs, deputy director of the Institute of State and Law of the USSR Academy of Science, I learned that books published by the Institute must be approved only by its Scientific Council. Censorship is exercised only with respect to questions involving national security. Where such questions arise, the manuscript is submitted by the Scientific Council for approval. Textbooks, I was told, are submitted to the Ministry of Higher Education, and those approved are designated as standard texts. Others, however, may be and are published at the discretion of the Institute and used in classes.

The much publicized book by Trofim K. Kichko, *Judaism Without Embellishment,* whose appearance was built into a *cause celebre* in the capitalist world, was published in Kiev in 1963 under the imprint of the Ukrainian Academy of Sciences. Its publication was approved on the recommendation of two individuals (both, incidentally, Jews) who were regarded as expert on the subject, and who wrote a foreword to it. Until the hue and cry arose the authorities in Moscow were entirely unaware of the book's existence. In this instance, when the matter was brought sharply to their attention the book was severely criticized and withdrawn from circulation. The editor responsible for allowing it to be published was removed from his position.

Thus it is that books or other writings with anti-Semitic implications or content are sometimes published in the Soviet Union. That any such writings should appear at all is, of course, regrettable. But it is clearly no proof of an official policy of publishing anti-Semitic literature. Such a charge can only be characterized as a malicious lie. Moreover, such writings are but a very minute fraction of the total Soviet literary output. Soviet readers are by no means flooded with anti-Semitic literature. Nothing remotely resembling the torrent of anti-Semitic filth which is freely printed and circulated in this country is to be found there.

Another alleged instrument of official anti-Semitism is the domestic passport which every Soviet citizen must carry from the age of sixteen on. Among other data, the passport states the nationality of the bearer and among the officially recognized Soviet nationalities is "Jewish." The purpose of this, it is charged, is to expose Jews to discrimination. Thus, Owen S. Rachleff, Director of the European Affairs Department of the Anti-Defamation League asserts that

> . . . the Jew must carry his label with him on the internal passport, a device which, we believe, is used by the USSR to foster anti-Semitism. Many Soviet Jews who have arrived in Israel report how extensively the passport must be used, and how it subjects them to backbiting, persecution and discrimination, simply because they are Jews. (*Hearings before the Subcommittee on Europe*, p. 203.)

We have already cited observers of the Soviet scene, including a spokesman of the State Department, to the effect that Soviet Jews are not persecuted as Jews. And even if individual acts of discrimination should occur, this would hardly prove that such was the *intent* of the Soviet government in listing "Jewish" as a nationality. (We shall deal with the statements and actions of certain Soviet Jews now in Israel in the next section.) In fact, no proof of such an allegation exists. The contrary is the case, as *New York Times* correspondent Peter Grose notes: "The word 'Jew' appears on official identity documents. This is a legal designation of nationality comparable to the designation Ukrainian, Latvian or Uzbek. Unlike the Hitlerian branding of Jews, *this in itself is not understood in the Soviet Union as discriminatory or derogatory.*" (October 27, 1967. Emphasis added.)

Concerning the meaning of the designation of nationality on Soviet passports the Novosti Press Agency states:

> At the time when the Soviet passport system was introduced there were proposals to specify only the Russian or a few of the most numerous nationalities, or to denote nationality according to the place of birth or domicile. These proposals were turned down since they objectively could be construed as disregard for other nationalities.
>
> A person's nationality is determined by the nationality of his parents regardless of the place of birth or domicile. . . . The bearer of the passport is free to choose the nationality of either parent.

Thus the Soviet passport is an important means of national identification. Specifying nationality betokens respect for the nation of its bearer. *(Soviet Jews: Fact and Fiction,* p. 46.)

To emphasize the truth of this last statement, it is enough to ask what would be the reaction of the "defenders" of Soviet Jewry if the Soviet government should declare that it no longer recognized the Jews as a national group and that henceforth no Jew could designate himself as "Jewish" on his or her passport. Would there not arise a loud howl that this constitutes an act of crass anti-Semitism designed to deny Jews their national identity? Truly, in the eyes of these people the Soviet Union is "damned if it does and damned if it doesn't."

2. SOVIET JEWS AND ISRAEL

Emigration to Israel: Soviet Policy

Today the anti-Soviet offensive is geared to the slogan "Let my people go." Not only are Soviet Jews persecuted in the Soviet Union, it is charged; they are also forbidden to leave in order to escape their persecution. Not only are Jews prohibited from "living as Jews"; they are also forbidden to migrate to Israel where they may do so. In this campaign the United Nations Universal Declaration of Human Rights is invoked, which assures to everyone the "right to leave any country, including his own."

If the bars to emigration were removed, it is alleged, there would be a mass exodus of Soviet Jews. Estimates range from 200,000 to the great majority of the USSR's 2,150,000 Jews. Sol Stern, writing in *The New York Times Magazine,* maintains that according to sources in the Jewish Agency in Israel, by April 1972 some 70–90,000 requests by Soviet families for *visovs* (invitations from "relatives") had already been processed, representing nearly 300,000 individuals. ("The Russian Jews Wonder Whether Israel Is Really Ready for Them," April 16, 1972.) A great upsurge of Zionism has taken place among Soviet Jews, it is said, and they are eager to depart.

So widespread is this belief that any challenge to it within the leading Jewish circles becomes an event. We have already noted the consternation created among Israeli Zionists by Nahum Goldmann's statement that most Soviet Jews would not leave the Soviet Union. And more recently, when Rabbi Irving Lehrman, president of the Synagogue Council of America, made a similar statement a fellow officer of the Council took note that this was "probably the first time that a responsible Jewish leader has stated clearly that the preponderant majority of the Soviet Jews wish to remain in the Soviet Union." *(Morning Freiheit,* May 7, 1972.)

But here, too, as with other anti-Soviet allegations, the wish is father to the thought. These enormously exaggerated estimates have no basis in fact, and no serious effort is made to substantiate them. Like the other falsehoods, they are simply repeated endlessly with the aim of gaining their acceptance as established facts.

The USSR Ministry of Internal Affairs, however, offers a more sober picture. In an interview in March 1972 *(New Times,* No. 16, 1972), Deputy Minister Boris Shumilin stated that up to 1971 some 11,000 Soviet Jews had migrated to Israel and in 1971 another 10,000 (substantially less than the 13–15,000 claimed by Israeli spokesmen). In 1972 the number was expected to be no greater. According to a Ministry spokesman, about four of every five applications for exit visas in 1971 were granted, which means that the total number applying to leave was not very much greater than the number who actually left. On this basis, therefore, at a rough estimate the total number of Soviet Jews desiring to go to Israel (including the recent departures) is somewhere in the neighborhood of one per cent of the Jewish population. The number itself is not much different from the number of U.S. Jews going to Israel to live (which also jumped considerably after 1967 and is now tapering off). And both are small.

Furthermore, those who wish to leave do not represent a cross-section of Soviet Jewry but are concentrated within certain narrow sectors of the Jewish population. In their great majority the applications for exit visas have come from two areas: the Baltic republics and Georgia. Georgians alone are estimated as accounting for as much as 40 per cent of the 1971 emigrants. On the other hand, from such major centers of Jewish population as Moscow and Leningrad, according to the Ministry, only 400 and 156 applications for exit visas, respectively, had been received since 1967. In addition, some two-thirds of the emigrants are older people.

The motivations for going to Israel are varied. Among the older generation, particularly in Latvia and Lithuania, there are those who want to be reunited with relatives living in Israel. Others are moved by religious considerations, especially among the Georgians. Still others are affected by bourgeois survivals (mainly in the Baltic republics, which did not become fully incorporated into the Soviet Union until the end of World War II) and by a desire to make money in business. In this connection *New York Times* correspondent Hedrick Smith notes: "Today, still, Georgian Jews are mostly small tradesmen and clerical workers. . . ." (December 1, 1971.)* And there are not a few who were influenced by Zionist propaganda. Among certain elements the 1967 war had a highly emotional impact, rendering them more susceptible to Zionist appeals. And such appeals have not been lacking, in the form of broadcasts from the Israeli radio station Kol Yisroel, dissemination of Zionist propaganda by tourists, a highly organized campaign of letters from "relatives" in Israel pleading with Soviet Jews to join them, and similar activities. "Come to your homeland, where you will be free to 'live as Jews,' " they were urged. These appeals were not without effect. However, those who succumbed were far fewer in number than the anti-Soviet crusaders would have us believe.

Finally, there are outright anti-socialist elements and shady characters of various types. *The New York Times* reports (January 23, 1972) that large numbers of the Soviet immigrants in Israel are

---

* Here the case of the Cuban Jews is highly instructive. At the time of the revolution there were 12,000 Jews in Havana and 2,000 more in other parts of Cuba. According to Lavy Becker ("Cuban Jewry Today," *World Jewry,* August 1971), this was a strongly Zionist-oriented community. After the revolution it was permitted the fullest freedom and facilities to carry on religious and Zionist activities.

But despite this ideal situation, today only some 1,400 Jews remain in Havana and another 450 in the rest of Cuba. Those who left have mainly gone not to Israel but to the United States. Why did more than 12,000 Cuban Jews find it possible to live under the Batista dictatorship but not in a socialist Cuba? The answer is clear: these were chiefly petty-bourgeois elements—businessmen, professionals and others to whom capitalism was preferable to socialism. Of course, this was not peculiar to Jews; other elements in these categories also left Cuba.

joining either the religious parties or the ultra-Right Gahal party headed by Menahem Begin. Many of the latter have also associated themselves with the Jewish Defense League. Among the leading lights in this group are Dov Sperling and Yasha Kazakov. Sperling was one of the "heroes" trotted out at the ill-famed Brussels conference for Soviet Jewry held in February 1971. On a trip to the United States, he appeared on David Susskind's television program with Meir Kahane and two other JDL leaders. On a tour of the country to solicit support for the anti-Soviet crusade, he and Kazakov also spoke at meetings organized by the JDL. And in Israel both have been vociferous supporters of the fascist ultra-Right elements.

A notorious example of the "shady character" category is one Grisha Feigin, another star performer at the Brussels conference. Feigin's story is that he was a World War II hero, twice wounded, once by a shell fragment in the head when he was 15 and once shellshocked when he was 18. He states that he flung his medals back at the Soviet government when his emigration to Israel was not expedited rapidly enough and that he suffered imprisonment for his Zionism.

The true story, however, is quite different. The records show that he was indeed imprisoned—once for two years for counterfeiting gold coins and once for one year for selling non-existent automobiles. At the age of 15 he was not in the army but living on a collective farm in the Tatar Autonomous Republic, far from any fighting. He was drafted at the age of 18 in 1944 but saw no action. He was never wounded and never received any medals. Nor was he, as he also claimed, a graduate of the Military Academy.

Feigin is by no means an isolated case. There are many more like him who have become Zionist "heroes." It is understandable why such people would want to get out of the Soviet Union. And it is clear that the crusade to "liberate" Soviet Jews has provided them with the opportunity to wrap themselves in a mantle of glory. But it is also clear that the perpetrators of this shameful crusade have no hesitation in using such criminal elements and renegades, and playing them up as heroic figures even though they are aware of their true character.

What is especially noteworthy in this picture is the comparatively small number who said they left because of anti-Semitic treatment in the Soviet Union. This in itself testifies to the falsity of the charges that Soviet Jews are subjected to persecution and terror.

The foregoing account, which is certainly far closer to reality than the fantasies of the would-be "saviors" of Soviet Jews, clearly belies the contention that the average Soviet Jew seeks only to get out in order to escape his torment. Nevertheless the clamor continues unabated. The mere fact that some 10,000 Soviet Jews migrated to Israel in 1971 rather than, say, 100,000 is offered as proof that no real loosening of restrictions has taken place. Furthermore, the Soviet Union is charged with harassment, intimidation and even imprisonment of those who demand the right to leave. The demand persists for the complete removal of all restraints on emigration, with repeated appeals to the UN Declaration of Human Rights to which, it is noted, the Soviet Union is a signatory.

It is true, of course, that the Soviet Union and other socialist countries follow a policy of restricting emigration, not only of Jews but of all citizens. Emigration is not regarded as an automatic right.

Why such a policy? One reason is the incessant efforts of the capitalist ruling circles and above all those of the United States, motivated by profound hostility to socialism, to undermine the economies of the socialist countries in every possible way. Among other things, they have striven to drain these countries of skilled, technical and scientific personnel, as well as to acquire a succession of emigrés and defectors to be used as propaganda instruments against the socialist lands. The CIA and other official agencies of subversion devote much of their energies to the achievement of these aims.

Under such circumstances, to allow unrestricted emigration would be fatal to the building of socialism. This the German Democratic Republic learned at great cost when the open border between East and West Berlin was used by the Bonn regime in a systematic campaign (financed with U.S. dollars) to plunder it of manpower, goods and finances. Only by building the Berlin wall and severely restricting emigration did it become possible to halt this and thereby to register the great achievements in the building of socialism which have since occurred in the GDR.

Secondly, in the socialist countries all higher education is free and in addition the students generally receive a stipend. Such education is not looked upon, as in capitalist countries, as something which an individual purchases and is then free to peddle to the highest bidder. On the contrary, it is viewed as something provided by the society to the individual as part of the process of social advancement for the benefit of all, and the individual is in turn considered as being obligated to use the education received for the benefit of the society. Hence he is not free to leave the country at will and to deprive it of the benefit of his knowledge. Indeed, anyone with such an outlook is regarded by others as a parasite seeking self-advancement at society's expense.

It is these considerations which underlie the decree issued by the Presidium of the Supreme Soviet of the USSR in mid-1972, requiring Soviet citizens who take up permanent residence abroad to reimburse the state for the cost of the higher education they have received. This action stirred the anti-Soviet crusaders to a new pitch of frenzy in which the Soviet Union was accused of no less a crime than "selling Jewish bodies." Space prohibits a detailed discussion of this question; however, the following points should be noted:

1. The decree applies not only to Jews but to *all* Soviet citizens. It is therefore not discriminatory.

2. There is, in addition to the UN Declaration of Human Rights, a pact approved by the UN and signed by a number of states which recognizes the right to restrict emigration on a number of specific grounds, including those involved here. In addition, Resolution 1,243 of UNESCO proposes measures by member states to restrict the drain of trained specialists by other states, including compensation for the financial losses caused. This resolution was prompted very largely by the constant drain of large numbers of scientific and professional personnel from the Latin American and other developing countries by U.S. imperialism—a practice which causes them considerable losses every year.

3. It is not uncommon for capitalist states to require repayment of debts, including debts to the state for educational purposes, as a condition of permanent departure. Israel, for example, has required immigrants wishing to return to their countries of origin to repay all funds advanced to them on their arrival as a condition for permitting them to leave.

The Soviet government has simply decided that it will not supply

Israel (or other capitalist countries) with trained specialists at the expense of the USSR. Such an action is in the best interests of the Soviet people.

Further, in the Soviet Union and other socialist countries every application for an exit visa is considered in the light not only of the desires and interests of the individual and the interests of the country as a whole, but also of the effect on international relations. This is especially important with respect to emigration to Israel, where it is necessary to take into account the situation created by the Israeli aggression and the interests of the Arab countries which are the victims of that aggression.

In the light of all these considerations the Soviet government has in past years permitted a limited amount of migration to Israel, mainly for the purpose of reuniting families. In 1971, as we have seen, the number permitted to leave was greatly increased. In fact, according to the Ministry of Internal Affairs, virtually everyone who applied for an exit visa received it, with the exception of people in certain specified categories. Among them are the following:

1. People with certain types of military training.

2. People whose departure, because of the nature of their occupations, would not be in the interests of the state. For example, those whose positions involve questions of national security are asked to change jobs for a time, then reapply.

3. People for whom no immediate substitutes are available. In such cases visas are delayed until replacements can be found.

4. Cases where the desire of some members of a family to emigrate threaten to break up the family. These are asked to settle matters among themselves before visas are issued.

Alleged "Persecution"

It is impossible to deal here in any detail with the countless allegations that Soviet Jews, especially those who speak up for their right to live as Jews or express a desire to go to Israel, are subjected to unceasing harassment and police surveillance—that they have been reduced to "Jews of silence" afraid to speak out. No doubt one can find Jews in the Soviet Union who maintain that this is the case, and there may well be instances in which for particular rea-

sons surveillance exists. But here suffice it to note that there are
also innumerable reports from visitors to the Soviet Union to the effect that the Soviet Jews whom they met spoke to them very openly
and freely and displayed no fear of harassment or intimidation of
any kind. Indeed, they often express anger at such stories, as they
do at the whole crusade to "save" them. As *New York Times* correspondent Peter Grose writes: "One can meet Soviet Jews every day
whose reactions to the foreign campaigns range from total bewilder-
ment to sincere anger." (October 27, 1967.) This is evidently the
case with the overwhelming majority of Soviet Jews; it is only a
small but vociferous minority, whose names appear repeatedly in
the various accounts, from which the tales of surveillance, loss of
employment and danger of arrest emanate.

Nor does space permit detailed discussion of the numerous allegations of unjustified imprisonment. We shall confine ourselves to
the most notorious of these: the case of the Leningrad hijackers.

From the very day the arrest of the twelve defendents in the case
became known, the campaign to brand the prosecutions as an anti-
Semitic frameup was under way. Typical of this barrage is the letter
to *The New York Times* (December 30, 1970) signed by Theodore
M. Hesburgh and other public figures, to which we have already referred. The defendants, it states, "were not accused of an actual hijacking or of a physical or violent attempt to hijack, or of actual or
planned violence of any sort." They were sentenced to prison or execution "merely for having discussed and planned emigration to Israel." Even more, says the letter, "their real crime, as one of them
puts it, 'was that they were born Jews and wished to remain Jews.' "

But the facts tell quite a different story. These people were arrested at the airport as they were preparing to board a plane with
arms in their possession and with the intention, as they themselves
admitted, of hijacking it. (And we have yet to hear of a non-violent
hijacking.) If they failed to carry out this act, it was only because
they were caught before they could do so. Moreover, they were
charged with seeking to leave the country illegally, which Soviet law
treats as a serious crime, and the basis of this charge was the attempted hijacking. The signers of the letter may not like this particular law, but this in no way lessens the right of the Soviet government to prosecute those who violate it.

In any case, the defendants *did* confess in court to attempting to hijack a plane, and this is regarded as a very grave offense not only by the Soviet Union but by virtually all other countries as well (in the United States it is a capital offense). This includes Israel—at least when the hijackers are Arabs, in which case no punishment is too severe. On more than one occasion, Israeli authorities have not hesitated to open fire on hijackers within the planes, even at the risk of the lives of the passengers.

However indefensible their actions, surely the motivation of Palestinian Arab hijackers—the freedom of their people—is no less noble than the desire of Jews to live in Israel (and the Arab refugees have as valid a claim as anyone to the right to live in Israel). Yet, in stark contrast to the vindictiveness against the Arab hijackers, when the criminals are Soviet Jews their prosecution becomes *ipso facto* the persecution of innocent people who want only "to remain Jews."

True, the death sentences imposed on two of the defendants were widely regarded as excessively severe and their commutation to lesser sentences was generally hailed. But this in no way justifies the demands that were raised for the freeing of all the defendants as innocent frameup victims.

The Disillusioned

What of those Jews who have gone to live in Israel? It is by now clear that there is much dissatisfaction among them and that many have come to regret their action and have returned or seek to return to the Soviet Union. No precise statistics are available but it is evident that the number who want to go back is far greater than a mere handful, as the Israeli authorities have claimed. According to some estimates, about 20 per cent have applied to return within a year of their arrival.

Among the religious Georgian Jews, much of the dissatisfaction is over their treatment with regard to religious matters. So serious has the situation become that in May 1972 one of their leaders, Rabbi Yehuda Butrashvili, came to the United States to alert the U.S. Jewish community to their problems. At a press conference he stated that "Georgian Jews who came to Israel to live a more religious life are finding it increasingly difficult to do so." *(New York Post,* May 18, 1972.)

Their chief complaint is the disruption of their communal life. They have a different religious tradition than the Ashkenazi or Sephardic Jews and they live in close-knit communities centered around their religious life. They have demanded, therefore, that they be settled in Israel in communities of 200 families or more and that special synagogues and schools be provided for them. They have complained that they are instead being dispersed, that their children are compelled to go to secular schools and that they have been compelled to work on the Sabbath. In fact, according to a story in the *Jerusalem Post Weekly* (February 15, 1972), some 200 Georgian Jews staged a demonstration at Lod Airport in protest against the dismissal of a number of Georgian Jews employed there for refusing to work on the Sabbath.

Not a few of them have concluded that they enjoyed more religious freedom in Georgia than in Israel and have decided to return. Thus, the *International Herald-Tribune* reported on November 27–28, 1971 that about 200 (it was not clear whether this meant individuals or families) had cabled Soviet President Nikolai Podgorny, asking for permission to return to the Soviet Union. And undoubtedly there have been others.

The main source of dissatisfaction, however, is the conditions of life encountered in Israel. Soviet Jews, accustomed to living in a socialist society, discover with a rude shock what it means to live under capitalism. In a speech to the Knesset, Communist member Emile Habibi states:

The Jews who come from the Soviet Union to Israel come very quickly to know matters, and they are perplexed. I have read what Georgian Jews now living in Affuleh have said, published in *Davar* of January 10, 1972:

Shabbetai Mikhalshvili, aged 31, reports that his material state in Tbilisi in the Soviet Union was very good. He had a flat of four rooms, central heating, all conveniences, gas and electrical appurtenances. No, he did not suffer from any anti-Semitism. He paid 2 rubles a month for rent of the house, all services included. His monthly wage was 220 rubles, which is more than 1,000 Israeli liras, and in addition he had all sorts of benefits. He was not only able in the Soviet Union to ensure the holiness of the Sabbath but also, and this is the main thing, to ensure the future of his children, their education and health, and all this at the expense of the socialist society. Here he is perplexed. He is still unemployed. There is no heating in his house. His wife works in a textile factory and receives 12 liras a day. (*Zo Haderekh,* February 16, 1972.)

Soviet Jews are indeed perplexed when they learn that they must now pay a high proportion of their income for rent and utilities, often for very inferior quarters, that they must pay considerable sums for health insurance, that they must pay for child care, for both high school and college education. And they are even more disturbed when they find they must work long hours at miserly wage rates for an employer who can fire them at will—that is, if they are fortunate enough to find work at all, let alone in their own trades or professions. And they express their dismay in the letters they write.

For instance, a letter sent by A. L. Cherches from Israel to the Soviet UN Mission in New York in March 1970, asking for help in returning to the USSR, says the following:

. . . I had been given an apartment, but I paid 150 pounds a month for it, besides 20 for electricity, 10 for gas, and 19 for water. Then, 30 pounds were deducted every month for the right to use the polyclinic. From 70 to 85 pounds a month went for bus fare. How much did all that add up to? More than 300 pounds. And for ten hours of work, after which I could hardly stand on my feet from fatigue, I was paid only 500 pounds a month.

Roughly, what remained: less than 200 pounds. That was barely enough to make ends meet, not to die of hunger, to preserve enough strength and energy to get through another shift the next day. And besides, I had to fawn on the boss, be grateful to him for giving me a job he could deprive me of any minute. In the Soviet Union, on the other hand, I enjoyed all the rights every other citizen did and slept tranquilly, knowing that my life did not depend on the whim of the boss, that the right to work was guaranteed me by the Constitution. (Quoted in B. Prahye, *Deceived by Zionism,* p. 43.)

Another letter, sent by Fishel Bender to relatives in Odessa, states:

An education is more than a poor person can afford in Israel. There is a tuition fee for all schooling beyond the eighth grade, and it's quite high at that. To attend a secondary school, for instance, it costs 70 Israeli pounds a month. Tuition fees are especially high when it comes to higher education.

But why talk about a university education. Even first aid is beyond the reach of the rank-and-file inhabitant of Israel. There are polyclinics in the country which cater only to those who contribute a definite sum every month to the hospital fund. Should you default on the next payment, you will be refused medical aid even if you have contributed regularly over a number of years and all the money you have paid in until then will be lost *(ibid., p. 55)*.

But this is not all. On arrival the Soviet immigrant, after initial processing, is assigned an apartment. However, the apartment most often turns out to be located not in an urban center like Tel Aviv or Jerusalem but in some development town in the Negev, miles from anywhere and devoid of cultural life. In many cases it is also far from the relatives whom the immigrant wants to rejoin. To Soviet Jews, accustomed to the availability of extensive cultural facilities, this is an added blow. It is worth noting that the Israelis themselves generally shun these towns; hence the availability of apartments in them.

In addition, the financial assistance given to the newly-arrived immigrant is mainly in the form of loans. These may cover his travel expenses in coming to Israel, expenses connected with obtaining and furnishing an apartment and other outlays. These are substantial sums which the immigrant is required to repay over a period of time. Should he change his mind and decide to return, as we have noted, he must repay the loans in full before he is permitted to go.

Finally, those Soviet Jews who migrate to Israel because they seek Jewish culture (which to them means Yiddish), quickly learn that nowhere is the use of Yiddish discouraged as it is in Israel. Some report that when they address questions to Israelis in Yiddish they are not infrequently told to speak Hebrew, not Yiddish. And they find that Yiddish theater, literature and music are at a low ebb. Yet the Zionist ruling circles conduct an all-out campaign to get Soviet Jews to go to Israel on the grounds that Yiddish culture is being stifled in the Soviet Union! What irony!

It is small wonder, then, that a growing flood of letters has been received by the Soviet Ministry of Internal Affairs and other agencies from Soviet Jews in Israel, pleading for permission to return. To be sure, the majority of the migrants can be expected to remain in Israel, but the desire of so many to go back testifies to the unquestionable superiority of the conditions of life for Jews in the USSR over those that prevail in Israel.

The important fact is that those who have sought to leave and on whom the anti-Soviet crusaders have based their clamorous propaganda are only a tiny minority. The overwhelming majority of Soviet Jews consider the Soviet Union their motherland and have no desire whatever to leave it. They are proud to be Soviet citizens, and in reply to the anti-Soviet slanders many of them have most emphatically said so. And with good reason. The transformation from the ghettoized and pogrom-ridden Jews of tsarist days to the Soviet Jews of today is little short of miraculous.

In tsarist Russia nearly 55 per cent of the Jewish working population consisted of traders, small shopkeepers, dealers and persons with no definite occupation. About 18 per cent were handicraftsmen, 11 per cent worked in cottage industries and 10 per cent were office workers. Only 4 per cent were factory workers and about 2 per cent were peasants. (*Soviet Jews: Fact and Fiction*, pp. 22–23.) Today, however, Jews work in all occupations. The so-called "Jewish occupations" are a thing of the past. The discrimination in employment and housing that one finds in the United States are absent. Jews live everywhere. There are no "Jewish neighborhoods," not even the "gilded ghettos" of U.S. suburbia. The flood of anti-Semitic filth and acts of desecration which so disfigure our country are unknown there; indeed, anti-Semitic acts and utterances are forbidden by law.

In a word, Soviet Jews enjoy a status of equality with other Soviet citizens which is unmatched in any capitalist country. More, they are citizens of a *socialist* country, working devotedly, side by side with others, to build the communist future for themselves, their children and their grandchildren.

This is the reality which the slanderers and detractors of the Soviet Union seek to distort or conceal. What is most shocking about their anti-Soviet campaign is not so much the endless succession of individual lies which they propagate; it is rather the all-encompassing Big Lie which presents a totally false picture of the status of Soviet Jews, of who are the friends and who are the enemies of the Jewish people, of where their real interests lie. Its dissemination and the campaigns of slander built on it do incalculable damage to the Jewish people themselves as well as to the cause of progress for all mankind.

3. THE SOVIET UNION AND THE MIDDLE EAST

The Issue Is Oil

We have noted above the Zionist charges that the policy of the USSR in the Middle East is to support those forces which seek the destruction of Israel and to arm the Arab states for that purpose. Underlying these is the proposition generally accepted in bourgeois circles that Soviet foreign policy, like that of the imperialist states, is based on the pursuit of power politics—of domination over other countries.

Soviet policy in the Middle East is treated as merely a continuation of tsarist policy. Its aims, it is asserted, are to secure warm-water ports, to protect the USSR's southern flank and to gain a foothold in Middle East oil. To achieve these aims the Soviet Union seeks to gain the favor of the Arab states, and toward this end it is prepared to countenance the annihilation of the State of Israel, which has been the steadfast purpose of these states. Such is the Zionist version. It is no less false than the allegations of "Soviet anti-Semitism."

In the Zionist view, the central conflict in the Middle East is that between Israel and the Arab states; hence, if the Soviet Union supports the latter it is *ipso facto* against the existence of Israel. But this is completely erroneous. The central conflict in this region, as it is in Asia, Africa and Latin America generally, is that between the forces of imperialism and those of national liberation. Here, as elsewhere, it is U.S. imperialism which is the chief protagonist of the imperialist forces, while the Soviet Union comes forward in support of the anti-imperialist forces.

The issue is oil. The Middle East has the most fabulous oil resources in the world. It contains two-thirds of the capitalist world's oil reserves and accounts for one-third of its production. The bulk of Western Europe's oil supply, and nearly all of Japan's, come from the Middle East.

Nearly the whole of this immense bonanza is in the hands of eight giant oil companies: Standard Oil (New Jersey), Standard Oil (California), Texaco, Gulf, Mobil Oil, Royal Dutch Shell, British Petroleum, and Compagnie Français des Pétroles. Five of the eight are U.S. firms; in fact, U.S. oil companies control more than 55 per cent of Middle East oil and British firms almost another 30 per cent.

Profits on these investments are the most phenomenal in the entire world. In 1965, reported profits of the U.S. oil companies on their Middle East operations averaged no less than 76 per cent of their stated investment as of the first of the year. The *Wall Street Journal* (March 14, 1966) reported that the 1965 pre-tax profits of Aramco, which controls the entire oil output of Saudi Arabia, amounted to 85 per cent on sales, as against an average of less than 10 per cent for all U.S. manufacturing corporations. Although investments of U.S. oil companies in the Middle East come to scarcely three per cent of total foreign investments, they account for 22 per cent of all repatriated profits on foreign operations. (*Survey of Current Business,* October 1968.) These fantastic profits are made possible by the extremely low production costs in the area, arising in part from the fact that the oil-bearing strata lie near the surface, but also in part from the fact that wage scales are among the lowest in the world.

It is the pursuit of these profits, as well as the strategic importance of the Middle East as a crossroads of the world, that has shaped U.S. policy there and has given rise to unceasing machinations designed to secure and expand the empire of the U.S. oil monopolies at the expense of their rivals and of the Arab peoples.

The history of the Middle East since World War II has been one of constant struggle and a succession of revolts against imperialist domination: in Egypt, Yemen, Syria, Iraq, Algeria, and more recently in Libya and Sudan. These states have freed themselves from their former colonial or semi-colonial status and some of them, notably Egypt and Syria, have taken the path of non-capitalist development and are moving in the direction of socialism.

The role of imperialism, and especially of U.S. imperialism, has been one of striving to stem and reverse the tide of revolt. In 1953 the Mossadegh government in Iran, which had nationalized the country's oil industry, was overthrown with the active involvement of the CIA. As a result the Anglo-Iranian Oil Company, which had held complete control of Iranian oil, was replaced by a consortium in which U.S. companies held a 40 per cent interest.

In 1955 the Baghdad Pact was engineered, with five official participants—Britain, Pakistan, Turkey, Iraq and Iran—and one unofficial participant: the United States. In 1959, after the withdrawal of Iraq, it was renamed the Central Treaty organization (CENTO). Its chief purpose was to deal with "subversive" activities in the region.

In 1956 there took place the ill-starred invasion of Egypt by Britain, France and Israel. In 1958, after the revolution in Iraq, U.S. troops were sent into Lebanon on the pretext of protecting that country from the threat of Iraqi attack. And in more recent years, U.S. imperialism has connived at the overthrow of the governments of Egypt and Syria.

Against Imperialism

Such is the basic contest of forces in the Middle East, in the context of which all other conflicts must be judged. The question is: for or against imperialist rule? The Israeli ruling circles, as we have shown in Chapter 3 above, have been consistently on the side of imperialism. And this has necessarily brought them into conflict with the Soviet Union and other socialist countries, which have been just as consistently on the side of the anti-imperialist forces.

When Czechoslovakia sold arms to Egypt in 1955, the purpose was not invasion of Israel (the cold facts are that Egypt has never invaded or even contemplated invading Israel), but defense of Egypt against attack. And Egypt *was* attacked, in 1956 and in 1967, and both times by Israel in collusion with imperialist powers.

The Soviet Union has not indiscriminately supplied arms to Arab states; it has done so only in the case of those countries which needed them for defense against threatened imperialist aggression, principally Egypt, Syria and Iraq. By the same token, U.S. imperialism has supplied arms to those Arab countries with the most reactionary, pro-imperialist regimes, such as Saudi Arabia and Jordan.

The Soviet Union has also given considerable economic aid to Arab countries, in the form of long-term loans at extremely low rates of interest and of generous technical assistance. The most prominent example is the aid given in construction of the giant Aswan Dam in Egypt. Syria is similarly receiving assistance in the construction of a series of dams on the Euphrates River. In short, Soviet policy is to give all possible help to Arab countries seeking to ensure their independence, political and economic, and to develop modern industrial economies.

With regard to the Middle East oil resources, the Soviet Union is charged with pursuing its own policy of "Soviet imperialism." But there is no such thing. In Soviet society there are no private corporations, no private investments, no private profits. The Soviet government's only interest is to help the oil-producing countries to free themselves of foreign exploitation and to develop their resources for their own benefit. In addition it purchases a limited amount of oil. (Actually the Soviet Union is an exporter of oil, mainly to other socialist countries.)

That this is indeed the role of the Soviet Union is recognized by even so conservative a publication as *U.S. News and World Report.* An article in its issue of June 26, 1972 notes that in Libya it has an agreement to provide technical assistance and is buying some oil from the nationalized oil fields; in Egypt and Syria it has long-term agreements to assist in explorations for oil and gas; in Iraq it has aided in developing the nationalized oil fields in North Rumaila and purchases some oil (and will undoubtedly aid in developing the more recently nationalized oil fields in Kirkuk); in Iran it also gives assistance in developing gas and oil fields and imports natural gas.

Again, the Soviet Union is on the side of the forces of political and economic independence in the Middle East, and it is precisely for this reason that its policies are anathema to the forces of oil imperialism and their supporters.

The attitude of the Soviet Union toward Israel is equally clear. Not only was it instrumental in bringing about the establishment of the State of Israel; it also supplied the new-born state with arms in defense of its independence. And since 1948 the Soviet Union has firmly upheld the rights of *all* states in the Middle East. It has opposed not Israel's right to exist but the aggressive policies of its leaders. This was made plain by Soviet Premier Kosygin in his speech before the UN General Assembly on June 19, 1967. He said:

. . . The Soviet Union is not against Israel—it is against the aggressive policy pursued by the ruling circles of that state.

In the course of its 50-year history, the Soviet Union has regarded all peoples, large or small, with respect. Every people enjoys the right to establish an independent national State of its own. This constitutes one of the fundamental principles of the policy of the Soviet Union.

It is on this basis that we formulated our attitude to Israel as a State, when we voted in 1947 for the UN decision to create two independent states, a Jewish and an Arab one, in the territory of the former British colony of Palestine. Guided by this fundamental policy the Soviet Union was later to establish diplomatic relations with Israel.

While upholding the rights of peoples to self-determination, the Soviet Union just as resolutely condemns the attempts by any State to conduct an aggressive policy towards other countries, a policy of seizure of foreign lands and subjugation of the people living there.

Soviet condemnation of Israeli aggression has been sharp indeed but, we maintain, it has been fully warranted, and in its stand the Soviet Union has performed a service in the cause of peace. Nor have its efforts for peace been one-sided; it has worked also to restrain threats to peace from the Arab side, as even Zionist spokesmen have felt obliged to admit.

Thus, at the annual Policy Conference of the American-Israel Public Affairs Committee in early 1967, a panel of experts discussed the Soviet role in the Middle East. *Israel Horizons* (February 1967) reports their conclusions as follows: "These men were in full accord that Russia did not want a war and would do everything possible to prevent one, and would step in very quickly to stop it if one developed. Moscow is evidently making this clear to the Arabs themselves, and especially to Syria. . . ."

These words are almost prophetic. The Soviet Union did in fact do everything possible to avert war in the Middle East in the only way it could be averted—by exposing and combatting the aggressive policies of the Israeli ruling circles, as well as by seeking to prevail on certain forces within the Arab countries to exercise restraint. In the explosive situation on the eve of the 1967 war the Soviet ambassadors in Cairo and Tel Aviv called Nasser and Eshkol, respectively, in the small hours of the morning to obtain assurances from each that his side would not be the one to fire the first shot. And when war broke out nevertheless, a war which served the interests of neither the Arab nor the Israeli peoples but only those of imperialism, the Soviet Union made every effort to bring it to the quickest possible end, pressing for an immediate cease-fire.

The danger of war in the Middle East persists, thanks to the annexationist policies of Israel's rulers in league with U.S. imperialism. The chief roadblock to peace is the adamant refusal of the Israeli government to commit itself to withdrawal from the conquered territories, in keeping with the UN Security Council Resolution of November 1967. Insistence on retaining these territories leads not to peace, not to security for the Israeli people, but to mounting hostility and the ever-present threat of the flareup of full-scale warfare with all its deadly implications. The road to peace lies only in abandonment of this policy, in accepting the UN resolution in its totality as Egypt, Jordan and Syria have already done.

The Soviet Union stands in the forefront of those who press for Israel's acceptance of the resolution and abandonment of its expansionist policy. In doing so, it continues to work for peace in the Middle East and for the best interests of all its peoples, Jews and Arabs alike.

VI

THE STRUGGLE AGAINST ZIONISM

Zionism vs. The Jewish People

To sum up, Zionism must be regarded as a deadly enemy of the best interests of the Jewish people and of working people in general. It is an enemy of peace, freedom and progress everywhere. It must be thoroughly exposed and its poisonous influence on the Jewish masses abolished. Moreover, an end must be put to the pro-Zionist mythology which has been so diligently cultivated among the people of the United States as a whole.

But one should not make the mistake of equating Zionism with the Jewish people. The masses of Jewish people, mainly working people, who join the various Jewish organizations and take part in their fund-raising and other activities, are not consciously Zionist in their thinking. Rather, they are motivated by such feelings as a sense of national pride and an emotional attachment to Israel, as well as apprehension for the future of the Jewish people growing out of the frightful experiences of the Hitler period. In themselves, these are natural and healthy sentiments; however, they have been perverted by the Zionist Establishment and harnessed to the support of reactionary policies both in Israel and in this country, policies which are falsely identified with the interests of Israel and the Jewish people.

At the time of the 1967 war there was an intense emotional reaction on the part of great numbers of Jewish people to what they saw as a threat of literal annihilation of Israel—a reaction which was built up to a pitch frequently bordering on hysteria. Consequently the influence of Zionism grew considerably, and there is no doubt that today it is easily the most powerful force in the Jewish community. But the Jewish masses, precisely because of the genuine concern among them for the future of Israel, can be won away from Zionist influence. As the annexationist policies of Israel's rulers and the disaster they hold in store for Israel are increasingly exposed, opposition to them will inevitably mount. Indeed, there are already significant beginnings in this direction.

The Peace Movement in Israel

Within Israel there is a growing questioning of government policy and a rising opposition is emerging. In its vanguard is the Communist Party of Israel, led by Meir Vilner and Tawfiq Toubi, which has consistently opposed the pro-imperialist, annexationist policies of the Israeli government and has condemned the 1967 war as an act of aggression. For a time it stood almost totally alone, but today opposition to one or another aspect of the government's line is developing in other circles. There is opposition to the occupation and to the policy of annexationism through accomplished facts. There are growing calls for implementation of UN Resolution 242, including withdrawal from the occupied territories.

These peace forces include a number of organizations and groupings, among them the "Ha'olam Haze-Koah Hadash" movement led by Uri Avnery, as well as a split-off group headed by Shalom Cohen; the Union of the Independent Socialist Zionist Left, consisting of former members of Mapam; Siah (New Israeli Left), established mainly by former youth members of Mapam; the Movement for Peace and Security, embracing varied groups and individuals and with a number of public actions to its credit, but recently infiltrated by elements seeking to convert it into a cover for government policy. Many prominent individuals have spoken out; thus, in December 1971 a group of 35 professors and public figures addressed a telegram to Prime Minister Golda Meir expressing a "feeling that as yet Israel's Government has not made the most of all its political possibilities to commence negotiations with Egypt" and calling on the government to "re-examine its declared positions." A substantial body of peace activists has developed among the youth, who have organized demonstrations and other protest actions. Student groups have accused the government of blocking a settlement, and there have been refusals to serve in the armed forces in the occupied territories.

These growing forces of opposition represent something new and vital in the Israeli picture. Still lacking, however, is unity of action among them. What is most urgently called for is the formation of a united peace front, rejecting anti-Communism and bringing together all peace forces regardless of their stand on the 1967 war. Given such a development, the peace movement can become a powerful factor for bringing about a basic change in Israeli foreign policy.

Opposition to Zionism in the U.S.

In the United States, too, opposition to the present Israeli policies is emerging within the Jewish community. However, it has yet to find organized form or suitable means of expression, thanks largely to the censorship and intimidation imposed by the top Zionist leadership, which exercises a tight control over press and funds and continues to insist that any criticism of the Israeli government whatever is a betrayal of Israel. Almost literally nothing is reported in the Jewish press of the opposition movements in Israel, and there is complete silence about such matters as the outrages committed by the Israeli authorities in the occupied territories. Nevertheless, signs of opposition are appearing even within Zionist circles, expressed partly in the form of protests against the rigid censorship.

Opposition has appeared especially among sections of the Jewish youth. Some, gravitating toward the New Left, have taken a distinctly anti-Zionist position. But others, even among Zionist youth, have also been affected. Having become involved in peace and Black liberation struggles, these young people have been subjected to the process of radicalization taking place among many sections of the people today, and have found their radicalism coming more and more into conflict with their Zionism. These tendencies find expression in opposition to the annexationist policies of the Meir government and in manifestations of sympathy with Left and opposition groups among Israeli youth.

Among non-Jews, support for the Zionist position has been declining. The Zionists' demand for unreasoning support to the policies of the Israeli government and their labelling of all opposition as anti-Semitic have helped to alienate growing sections among gentiles. Particularly noteworthy has been the challenge to the Zionist stand among Christian religious groups.

An outstanding example is the study *Search for Peace in the Middle East,* published by the American Friends Service Committee in 1970 and revised later that year. Prepared by a Quaker-sponsored committee of various religious denominations and released at the United Nations, the study is sharply critical of Israeli policies, though it is at the same time not uncritical of Arab policies. However, it stresses the need of a change in the Israeli position if peace in the Middle East is to be achieved, saying:

It is the judgment of the authors of this paper that without certain first moves by Israel, which only the militarily dominant power can make, progress toward a settlement of the Middle East situation cannot be made. Those first moves should involve firm public commitments to withdraw from Arab territories as part of a comprehensive peace settlement and to aid in the search for positive solutions to the Palestinian refugee problem (pp. 114–15).

With regard to the situation in leading Jewish circles in this country it states:

Our impression, confirmed by many comments from Israelis inside Israel, is that there is a tendency for some of the leaders of the American Jewish establishment to identify themselves with the more hard-line elements inside the Israeli cabinet, and to ignore or discount the dissident elements, in and out of the Israeli government, that are searching for more creative ways to solve the Middle East problem.

It calls upon U.S. Jewish leaders to reassess the nature of their support to the Israeli government (pp. 116–17).

Needless to say, the Quaker study has greatly aroused the ire of the Zionist Establishment, which has gone out of its way to attack it. However, it offers the basis for a serious challenge to the Zionist position.

These and other expressions of opposition which are developing are, of course, not directed against Zionism as such; in fact, they arise mainly within the framework of acceptance of the premises of Zionism and take issue only with certain specific policies of the Israeli government. But such policies, as we have sought to show in these pages, stem directly from the precepts of Zionism. A basic change in policy and direction for Israel, therefore, requires the abandonment of these precepts and the conclusions flowing from them. If the movement against the present policy of aggression is to grow and to acquire effective organized form, it is essential to lay bare the reactionary bourgeois-nationalist character of Zionism and its domination by big Jewish capital in league with U.S. monopoly capital as a whole.

A fight must be waged against the idea of Israel as the state of all the Jewish people and of Jews exclusively, and for an Israel conceived of as the land of the Israeli people—a land of full equality of all Israeli citizens, whether Jew or Arab, Western or Oriental. It is necessary to fight for an Israel which will become part of the Middle East and will seek its ties not with the forces of imperialism which oppress the Arab peoples but with the anti-imperialist forces among the Arabs. It is necessary to strive for Israeli independence of foreign monopoly capital, for economic relations with the socialist countries, and for the achievement of economic independence as the only foundation for a viable economy and a secure future. It is necessary to press for recognition of the right of self-determination of the Palestinian Arabs, including a just solution of the refugee question. It is necessary, in a word, to fight for the de-Zionization of Israel. The unfolding of such struggles is the task of the Israeli people in the first place—but not of the Israeli people alone.

In the United States—the heartland of world imperialism and the home of the world's largest Jewish community—the fight against Zionism takes on exceptional importance. It is here, above all, that the dangerous machinations of U.S. imperialism in the Middle East must be combatted. It is here, next to Israel itself, that the pressures to compel a basic change in Israeli foreign policy must be generated. And it is here that the struggle against the slanderous attacks on the Soviet Union and other socialist countries must be focused.

The great hoax perpetrated by Zionism on the Jewish people—indeed, on all the people of our country—can and will be exposed. The eradication of Zionist influences will mark a big step forward for the Jewish people. It will permit them, in Israel and in other countries, to turn their creative energies in more fruitful directions. It will go far toward freeing them of racist and chauvinist influences. It will open up the way toward Jewish-Arab brotherhood and peace in the Middle East. And it will contribute greatly to securing world peace.

BOOKS AND PAMPHLETS CITED

Africa Research Group, *David and Goliath Collaborate in Africa*, Cambridge, 1969.

American Friends Service Committee, *Search for Peace in the Middle East*, revised edition, Fawcett Publications, Inc., Greenwich, 1970.

Uri Avnery, *Israel Without Zionists: A Plea for Peace in the Middle East*, Macmillan, New York, 1968.

Michael Bar-Zohar, *Ben-Gurion: The Armed Prophet*, Prentice-Hall, New York, 1968.

Chaim Bermont, *Israel*, Walker and Co., New York, 1967.

Ber Borochov, *Selected Essays in Socialist-Zionism*, (S. Levenberg, ed.), Rita Searl, London, 1948.

Central Bureau of Statistics, *Income Surveys, 1965–1967*, Jerusalem, 1969.

Aharon Cohen, *Israel and the Arab World*, Funk and Wagnalls, New York, 1970.

S. M. Doubnow, *An Outline of Jewish History*, 3 vols., Max N. Maisel, New York, 1925.

Amos Elon, *The Israelis: Founders and Sons*, Bantam Books, New York, 1967.

Georges Friedmann, *The End of the Jewish People?*, Doubleday, New York, 1967.

Irene Gendzier, ed., *A Middle East Reader*, Pegasus, New York, 1969.

Frank Gervasi, *To Whom Palestine*, Appleton-Century, New York, 1946.

Nahum Goldmann, *The Autobiography of Nahum Goldmann: Sixty Years of Jewish Life*, Holt, Rinehart and Winston, New York, 1969.

Sanford Goldner, *Perspectives in Jewish Life*, Ward Ritchie Press, Los Angeles, 1959.

Nadav Halevi and Ruth Klinov-Malul, *The Economic Development of Israel*, Praeger, New York, 1968.

Arthur Hertzberg, *The Zionist Idea*, Harper, New York, 1959.

Theodor Herzl, *The Jewish State*, Scopus Publishing Co., New York, 1943.

The Diaries of Theodor Herzl, Grosset and Dunlap, New York, 1962.

Moses Hess, *Rome and Jerusalem*, Philosophical Library, New York, 1958.

Ira Hirschmann, *Red Star Over Bethlehem*, Simon and Schuster, New York, 1971.

Aubrey Hodes, *Dialogue with Ishmael: Israel's Future in the Middle East*, Funk and Wagnalls, New York, 1968.

Jewish Agency for Palestine, *The Jewish Case before the Anglo-American Committee on Palestine as Presented by the Jewish Agency for Palestine*, Jerusalem, 1947.

Jewish Colonial Trust, *Survey of Activities and Financial Report, 1899–1922*, Financial and Economic Council of the Zionist Organization, London, 1922.

Meir Kahane, *Never Again!—A Program for Survival*, Nash Publishing, Los Angeles, 1971.

Shlomo Katz, ed., *Negro and Jew: An Encounter in America*, Macmillan, New York, 1967.

Fred J. Khouri, *The Arab-Israel Dilemma*, University of Syracuse Press, Syracuse, 1968.

Jon and David Kimche, *The Secret Roads: The "Illegal" Migration of a People, 1938-1948*, Secker and Warburg, London, 1954.

Leopold Laufer, *Israel and the Developing Countries: New Approaches to Cooperation*, Twentieth Century Fund, New York, 1967.

Hyman Lumer, *The "Jewish Defense League"—A New Face for Reaction*, New Outlook Publishers, New York, 1971.

A. B. Magil, *Israel in Crisis*, International Publishers, New York, 1950.

S. Menshikov, *Millionaires and Managers*, Progress Publishers, Moscow, 1969.

S. Novich, *In a Close-Knit Family of Nations*, Novosti Press Agency Publishing House, Moscow, n. d.

Paul Novick, *Jewish Life in the United States and the Role of the "Morning Freiheit,"* Morning Freiheit, New York, 1957.

Anthony Nutting, *No End of a Lesson*, Clarkson N. Potter, New York, 1967.

Don Peretz, *Israel and the Palestine Arabs*, Middle East Institute, Washington, 1958.

Victor Perlo, *The Empire of High Finance*, International Publishers, New York, 1957.

Leo Pinsker, *Auto-Emancipation*, Zionist Organization of America, New York, 1944.

B. Prahye, *Deceived by Zionism*, Novosti Press Agency Publishing House, Moscow, 1971.

Solomon Rabinovich, *Jews in the Soviet Union*, Novosti Press Agency Publishing House, Moscow, 1967.

Bert Ramelson, *The Middle East: Crisis, Causes, Solution*, Communist Party of Great Britain, London, 1967.

Nadav Safran, *The United States and Israel*, Cambridge, 1963.

Michael Selzer, *Israel as a Factor in Jewish-Gentile Relations in America: Observations in the Aftermath of the June, 1967 War*, American Council on Judaism, New York, 1968.

Robert Silverberg, *If I Forget Thee O Jerusalem: American Jews and the State of Israel*, William Morrow and Co., New York, 1970.

Soviet Jewry: Hearings before the Subcommittee on Europe of the Committe on Foreign Affairs of the House of Representatives, Government Printing Office, Washington, 1972.

Soviet Jews: Fact and Fiction, Novosti Press Agency Publishing House, Moscow, 1971.

Chaim Weizmann, *Trial and Error: The Autobiography of Chaim Weizmann*, Harper, New York, 1949.